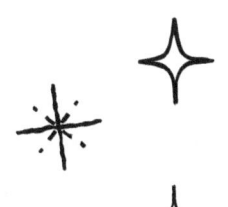

YOUR SIGN AS A
dessert

ARIES
chocolate chip cookies
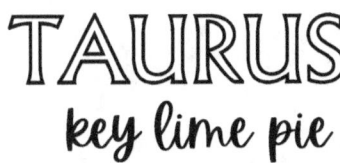

TAURUS
key lime pie
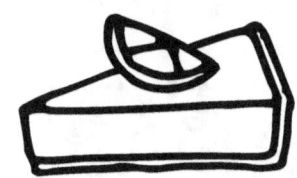

SAGITTARIUS
cupcake

LEO
brownies
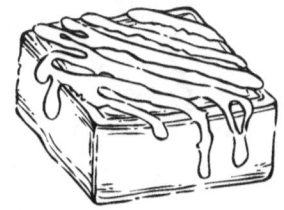

CANCER
cheesecake
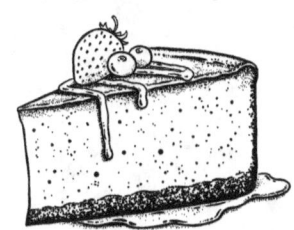

GEMINI
ice cream sandwich
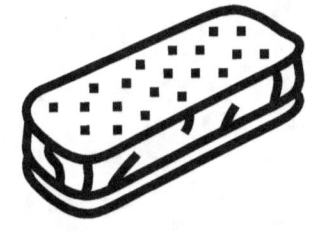

LIBRA
churros
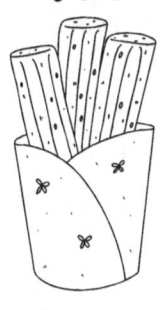

SCORPIO
cinnamon roll
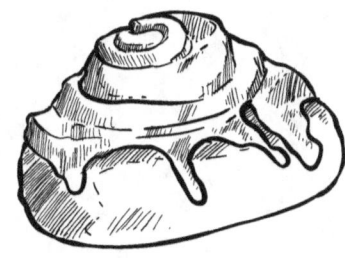

AQUARIUS
chocolate cake
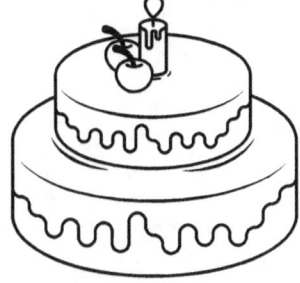

VIRGO
tiramisu
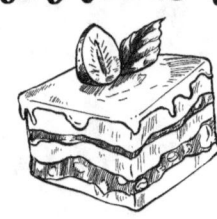

CAPRICORN
sprinkled donut
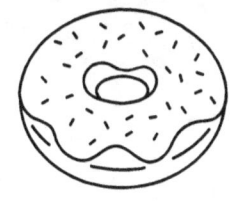

PISCES
mochi ice cream
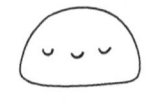 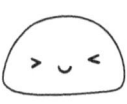 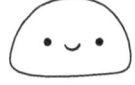

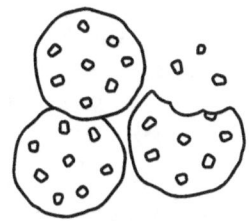
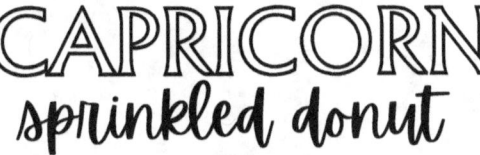

YOUR SIGN AS A *cocktail*

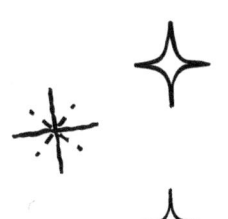
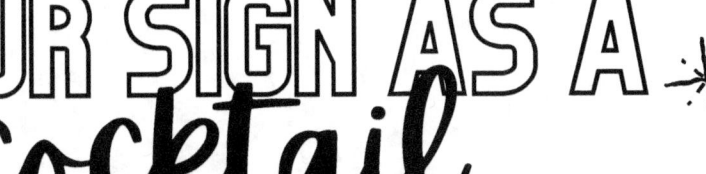
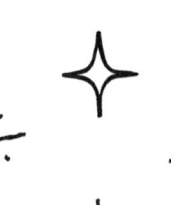

ARIES
bloody mary

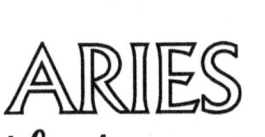

TAURUS
gin & tonic

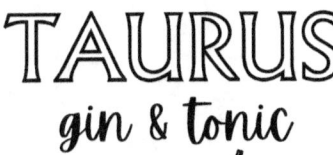

SAGITTARIUS
mojito

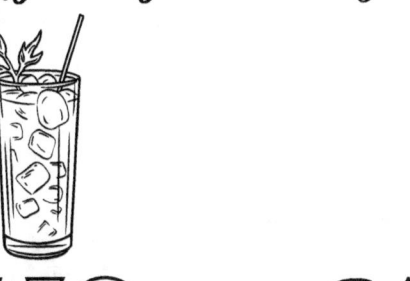
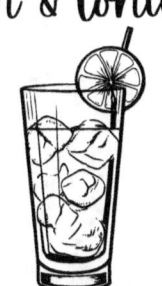
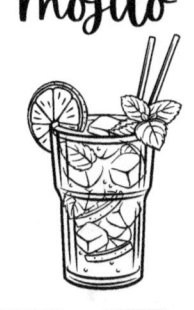

LEO
mimosa

CANCER
mai tai

GEMINI
french 75

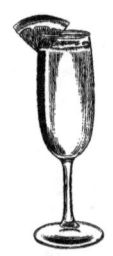
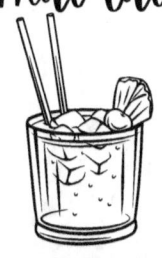
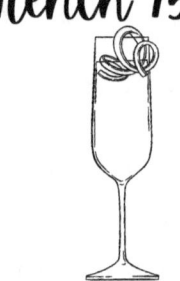

LIBRA
mint julep

SCORPIO
martini

AQUARIUS
negroni

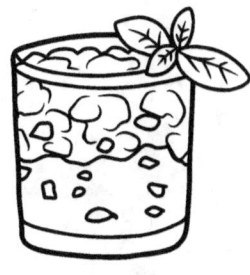
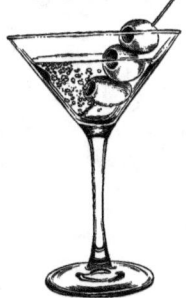
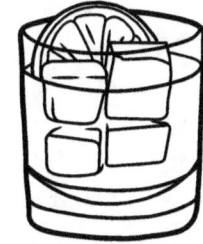

VIRGO
manhattan

CAPRICORN
old fashioned

PISCES
cosmo

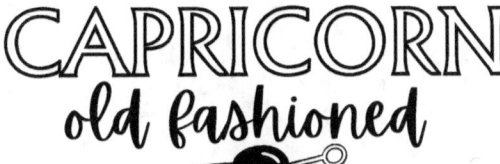
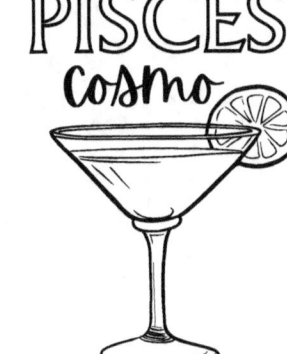
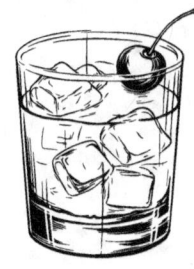
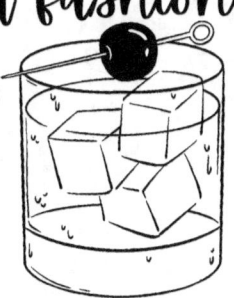

YOUR SIGN AS A
house plant

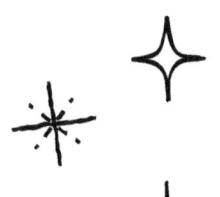 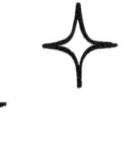

ARIES
cactus

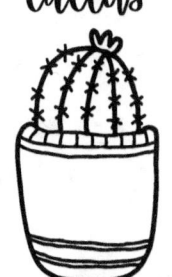

TAURUS
pothos

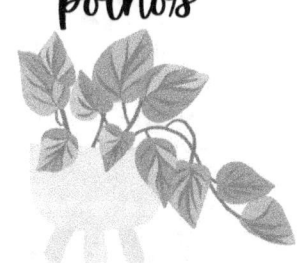

SAGITTARIUS
birds of paradise

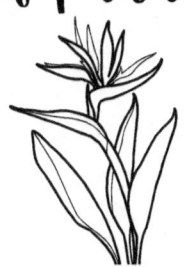

LEO
monstera

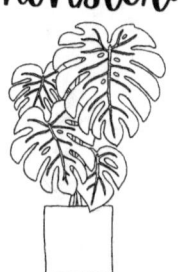

CANCER
spider plant

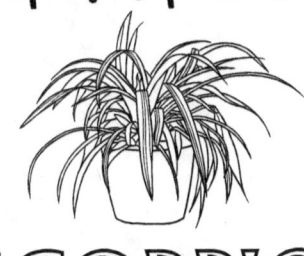

GEMINI
string of pearls

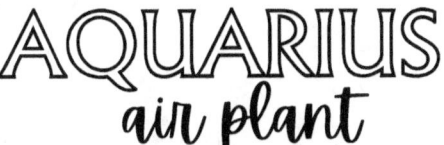

LIBRA
peace lily

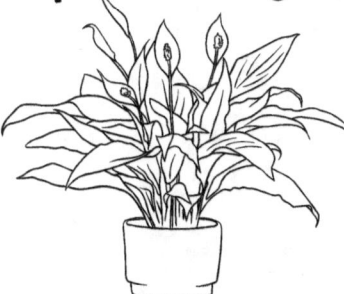

SCORPIO
snake plant

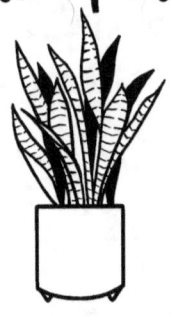

AQUARIUS
air plant

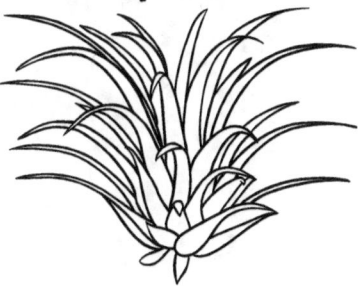

VIRGO
fiddle leaf fig

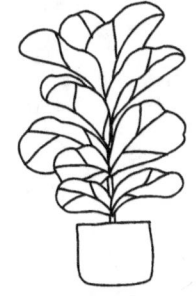

CAPRICORN
money tree

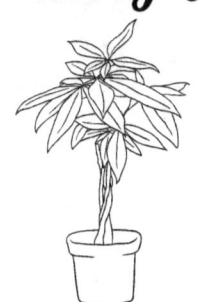

PISCES
aloe vera

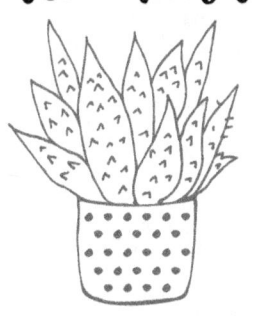

YOUR SIGN AS A
snack

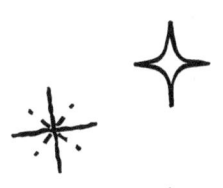
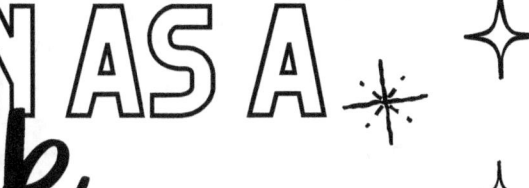

ARIES
cheese puffs

TAURUS
potato chips

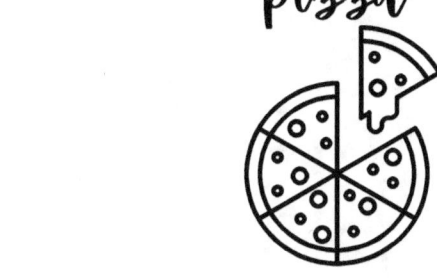

SAGITTARIUS
pizza

LEO
hot dog

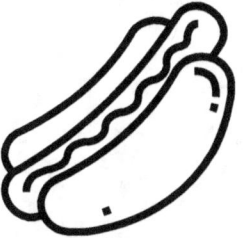

CANCER
cookies

GEMINI
nachos

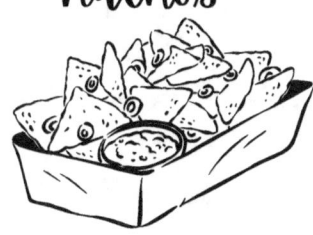

LIBRA
tacos

SCORPIO
chocolate bar

AQUARIUS
popcorn

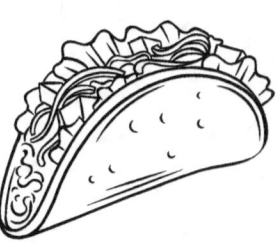
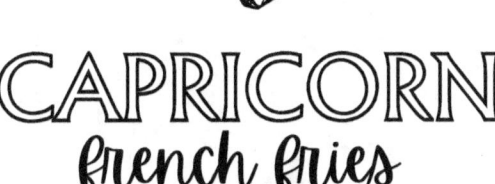
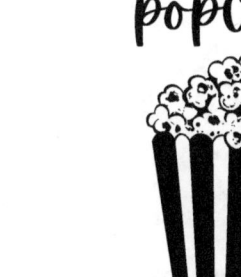
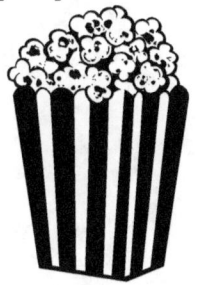

VIRGO
chicken nuggets

CAPRICORN
french fries

PISCES
ice cream cone

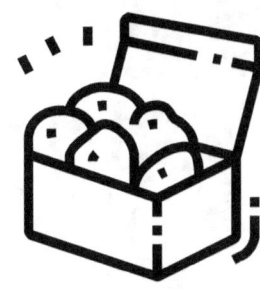
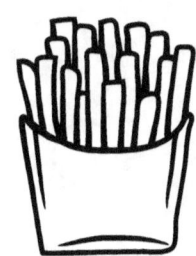
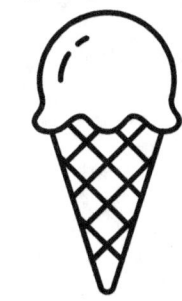

YOUR SIGN AS A
flower

ARIES
daisy

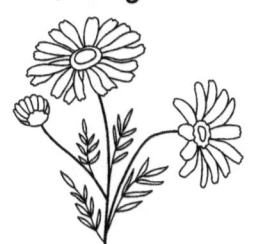

TAURUS
tulips

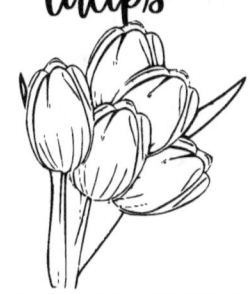

SAGITTARIUS
rose

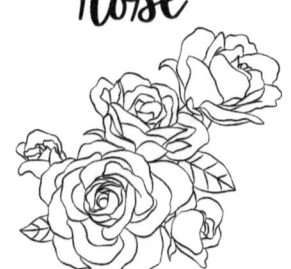

LEO
lavendar

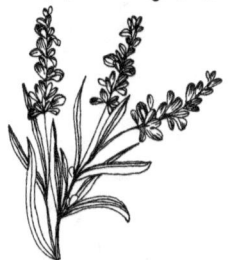

CANCER
hydrangea

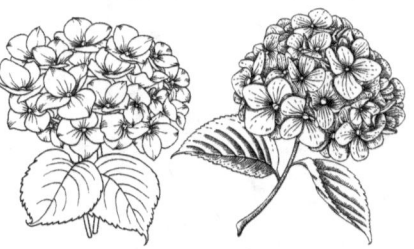

GEMINI
hyacinth

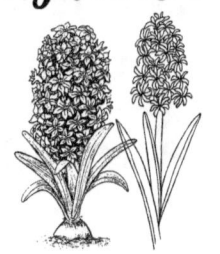

LIBRA
alliums

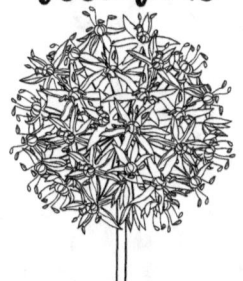

SCORPIO
primrose

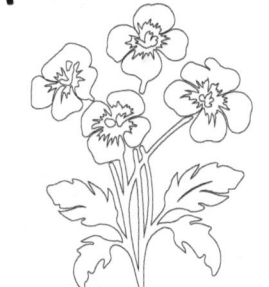

AQUARIUS
lily of the valley

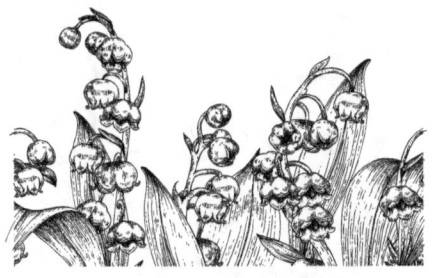

VIRGO
daffodil

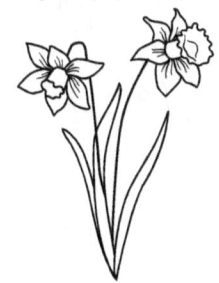

CAPRICORN
violas

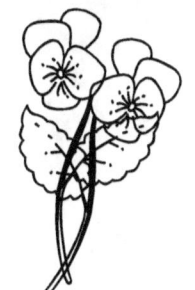

PISCES
sunflower

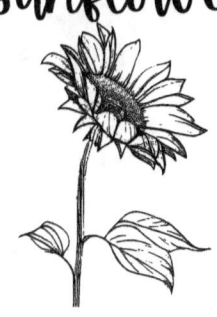

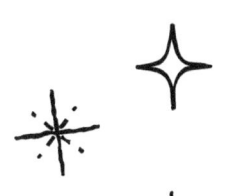

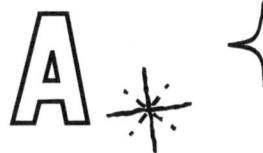

YOUR SIGN AS A
mug style

ARIES
future is female

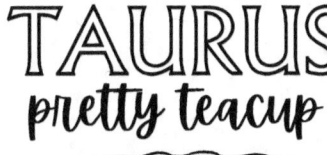

TAURUS
pretty teacup

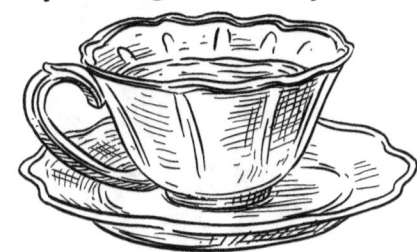

SAGITTARIUS
favorite cartoon character

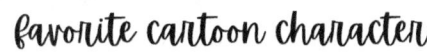
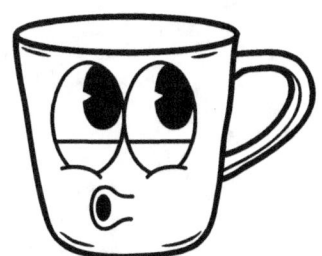

LEO
sloth mug

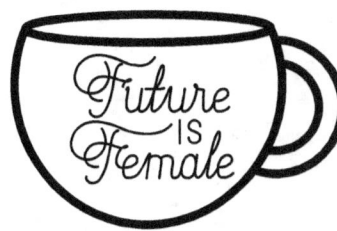

CANCER
*f*ck this*

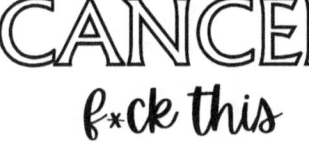
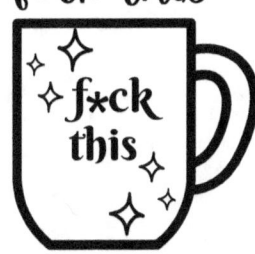

GEMINI
plain mug

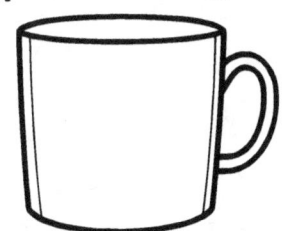

LIBRA
a political statement

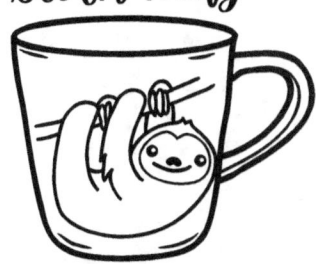

SCORPIO
hustle hard

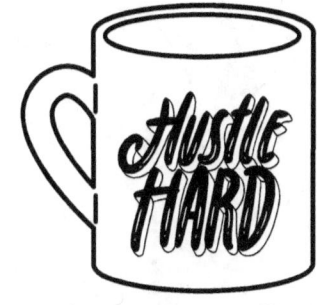

AQUARIUS
handmade ceramic mug

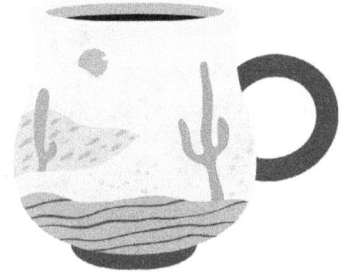

VIRGO
whole pot of coffee

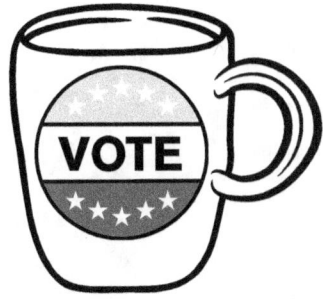

CAPRICORN
astrological sign

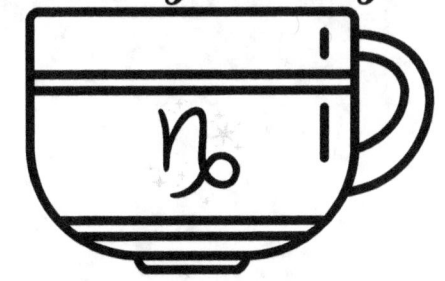

PISCES
photo of their pet

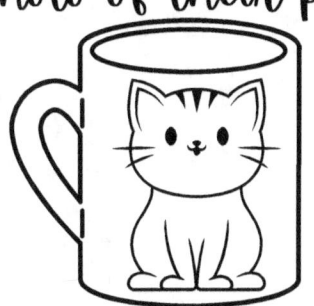
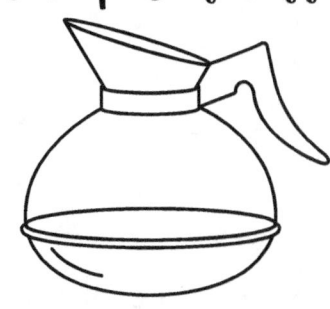

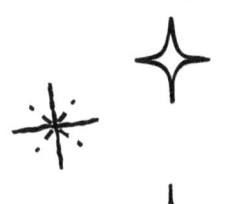
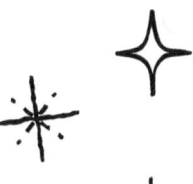

YOUR SIGN AS A
fruit

ARIES
strawberry

TAURUS
pomegranate

SAGITTARIUS
grapes
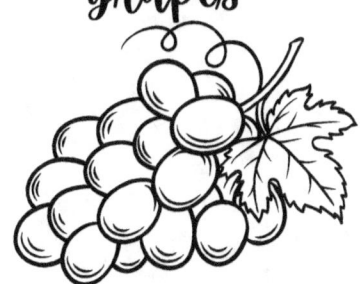

LEO
orange
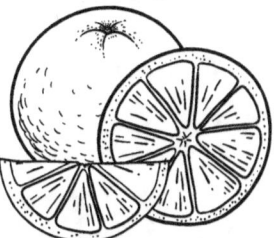

CANCER
pear
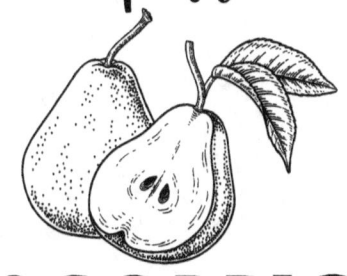

GEMINI
apple
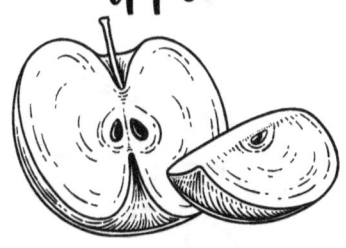

LIBRA
mango
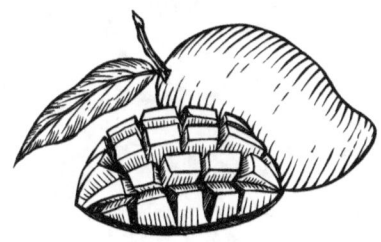

SCORPIO
blackberry
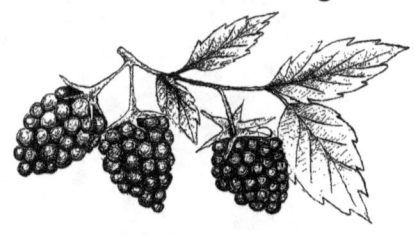

AQUARIUS
pineapple
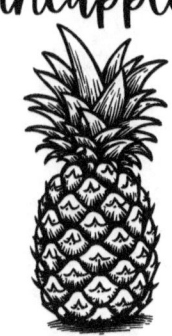

VIRGO
watermelon
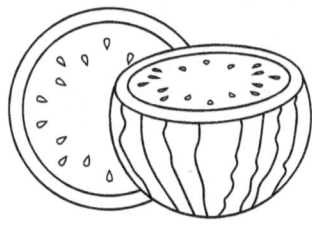

CAPRICORN
banana
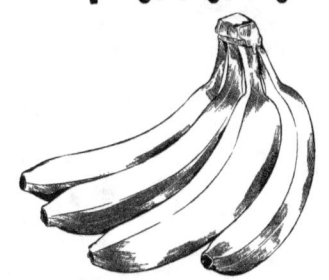

PISCES
blueberry

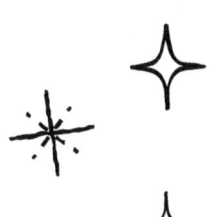

YOUR SIGN AS A
coffee drink

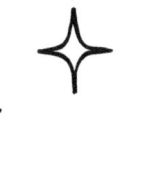

ARIES
peppermint mocha

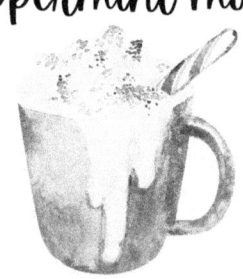

TAURUS
iced coffee

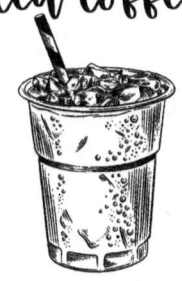

SAGITTARIUS
americano

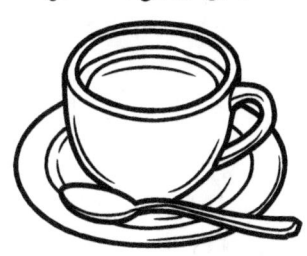

LEO
cappuccino

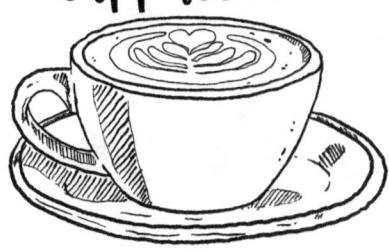

CANCER
caramel macchiato

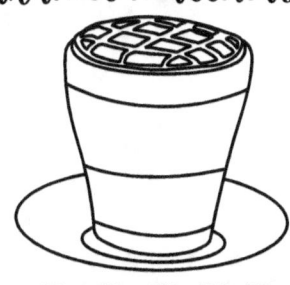

GEMINI
hot chocolate

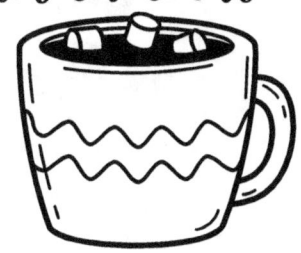

LIBRA
frappuccino

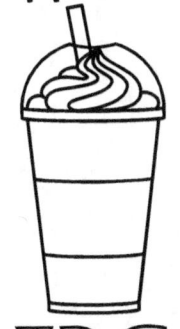

SCORPIO
black coffee

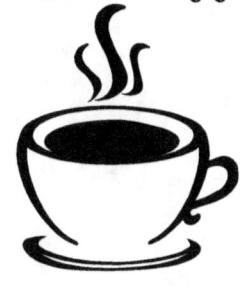

AQUARIUS
cold brew

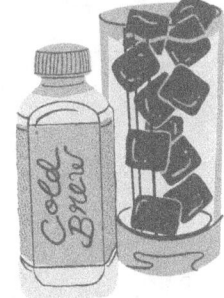

VIRGO
pumpkin spice latte

CAPRICORN
matcha

PISCES
chai latte

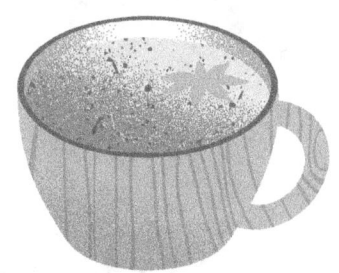

YOUR SIGN AS A
dog breed

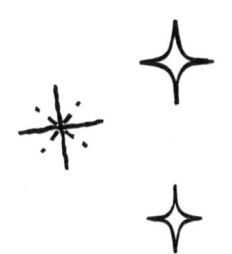
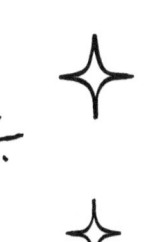

ARIES
chihuahua- moody

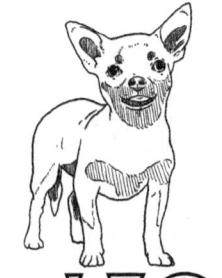

TAURUS
shih tzu- luxurious

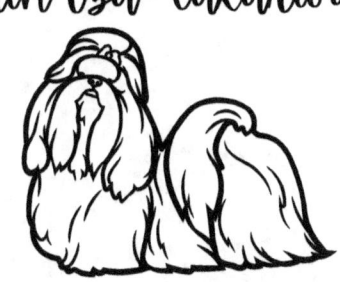

SAGITTARIUS
bull terrier- playful

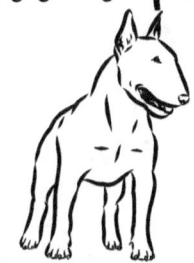

LEO
Pomeranian- diva

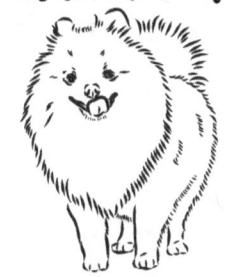

CANCER
Itlaian greyhound- gentle

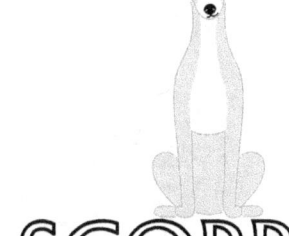

GEMINI
beagle- vocal

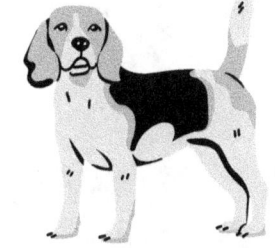

LIBRA
golden retriever- humorous

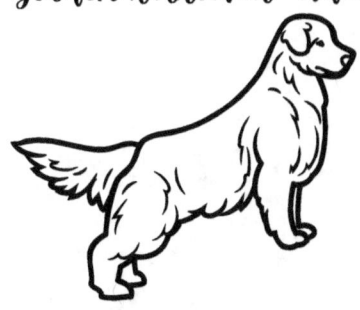

SCORPIO
french bulldog- possesive

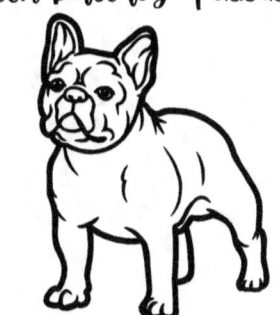

AQUARIUS
chow chow- aloof

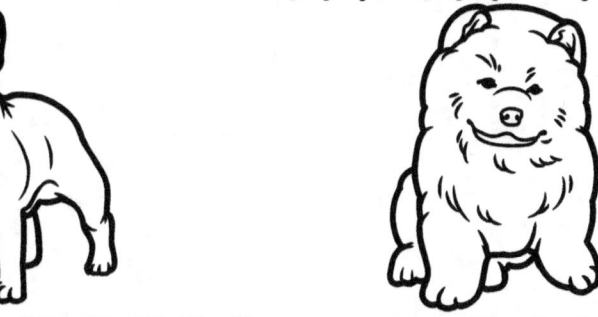

VIRGO
german shepherd- natural leader

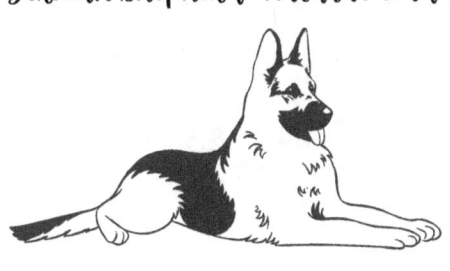

CAPRICORN
shiba inu- stubborn

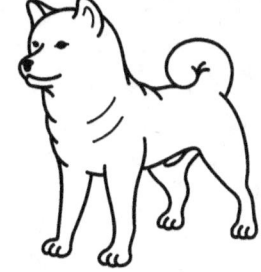

PISCES
cocker spaniel- sensitive

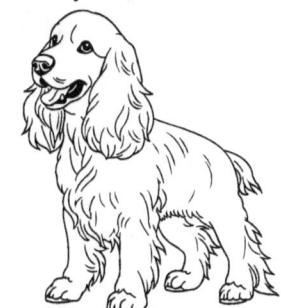

YOUR SIGN AS AN
ice cream flavor

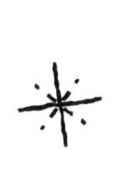 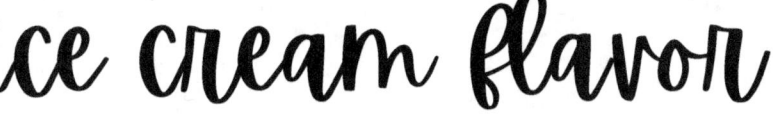 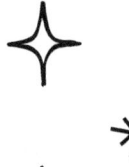 

ARIES
coffee

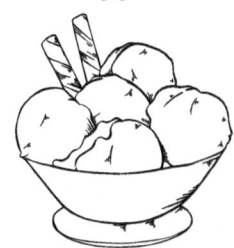

TAURUS
pistcahio

SAGITTARIUS
rocky road

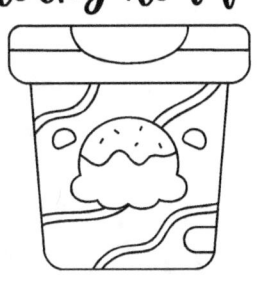

LEO
birthday cake

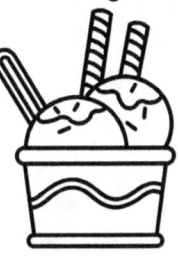

CANCER
cookies & cream

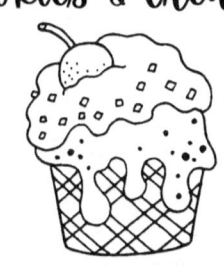

GEMINI
neopolitan

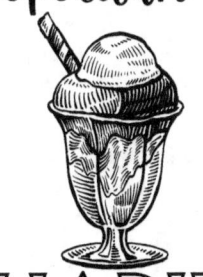

LIBRA
vanilla

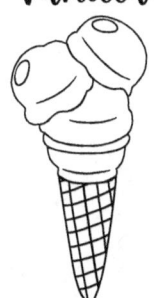

SCORPIO
chocolate

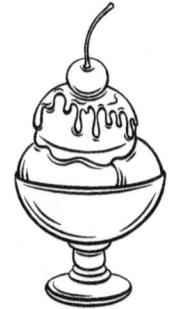

AQUARIUS
mint chocolate chip

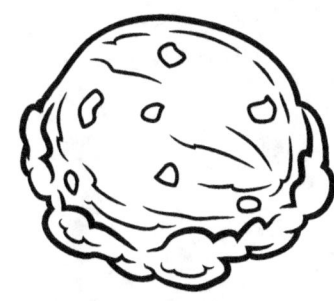

VIRGO
salted caramel

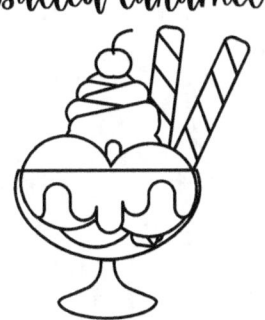

CAPRICORN
cookie dough

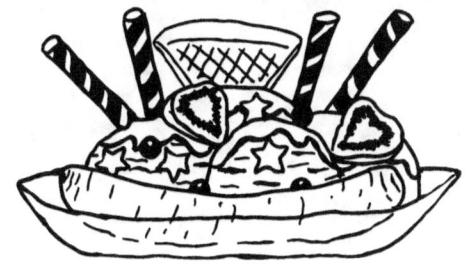

PISCES
butter pecan

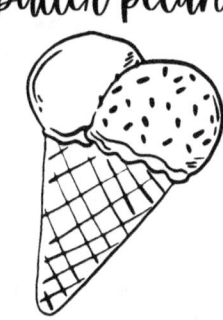

YOUR SIGN AS A
candy

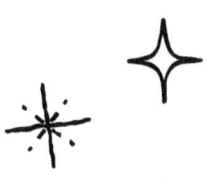

ARIES
hard candy

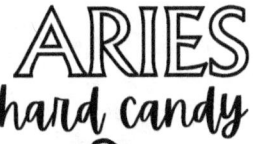

TAURUS
marshmallows

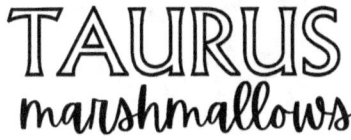

SAGITTARIUS
candy corn

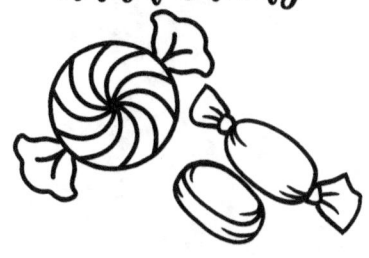
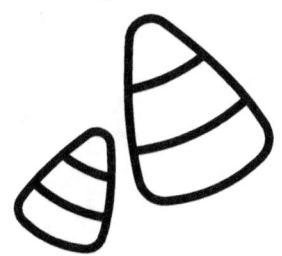

LEO
lollipops

CANCER
peanut butter cup

GEMINI
cotton candy

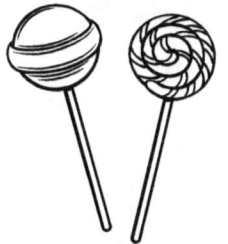
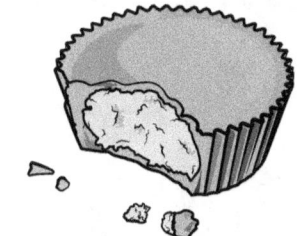
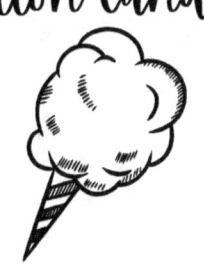

LIBRA
truffles

SCORPIO
licorice

AQUARIUS
gummy bears

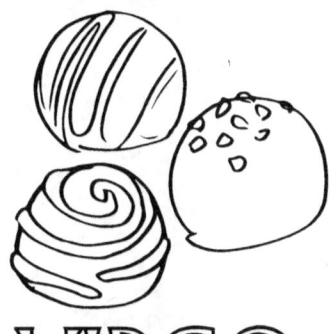
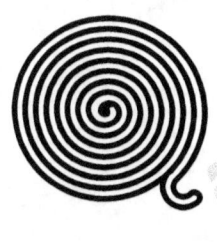
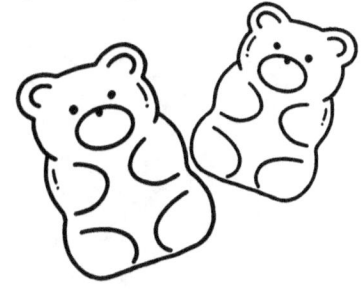

VIRGO
chocolate kiss

CAPRICORN
salt water taffy

PISCES
bubble gum

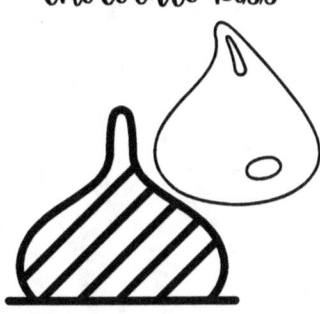

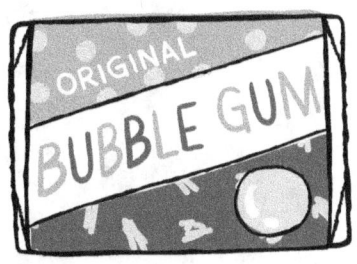

YOUR SIGN AS A
candle scent

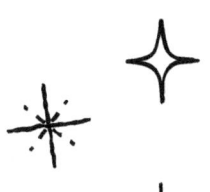

ARIES
sweet strawberry

TAURUS
midnight jasmine

SAGITTARIUS
balsam cedar

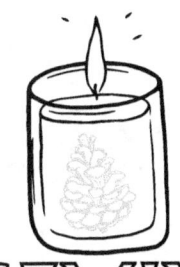

LEO
sun & sand

CANCER
vanilla cupcake

GEMINI
mimosa madarin

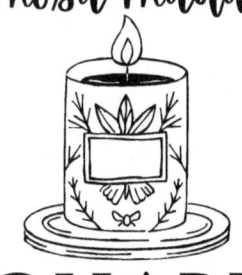

LIBRA
pink kiss

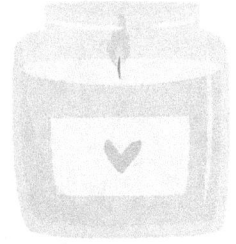

SCORPIO
cashmere

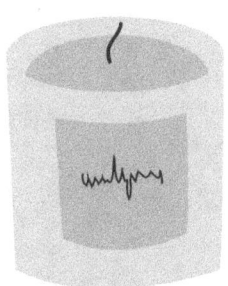

AQUARIUS
garden blossoms

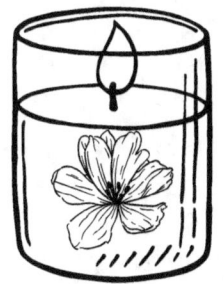

VIRGO
cinnamon stick

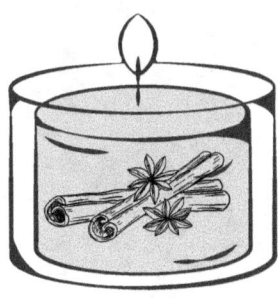

CAPRICORN
full moon above

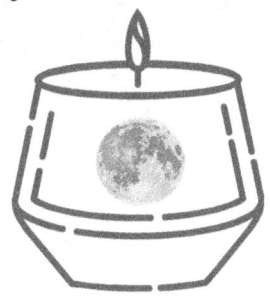

PISCES
magic spell

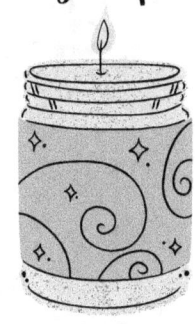

YOUR SIGN AS A
witchy tool

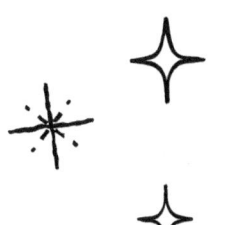

ARIES
mortar & pestle

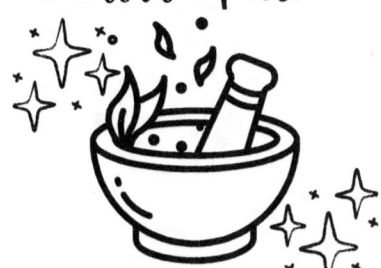

TAURUS
crystals

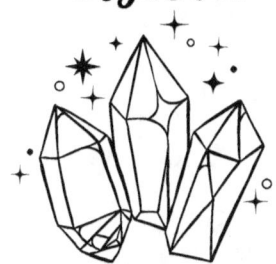

SAGITTARIUS
candles

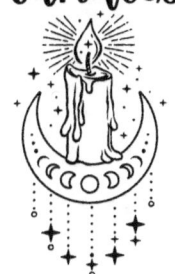

LEO
tarot cards

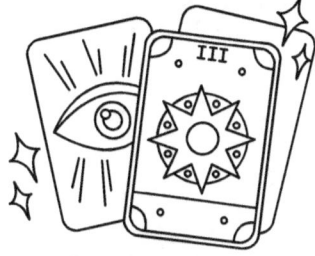

CANCER
book of shadows

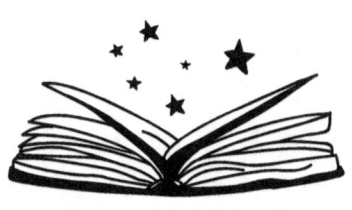

GEMINI
jars

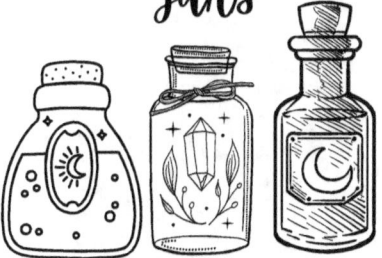

LIBRA
incense

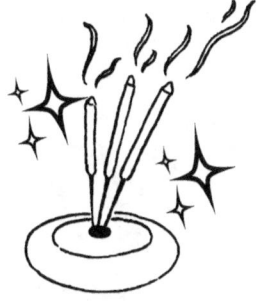

SCORPIO
broom

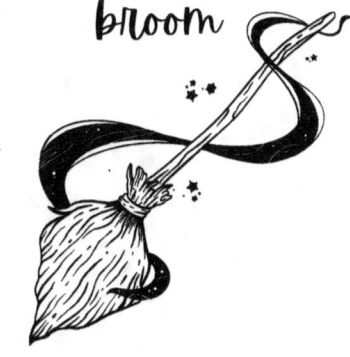

AQUARIUS
cauldron

VIRGO
wand

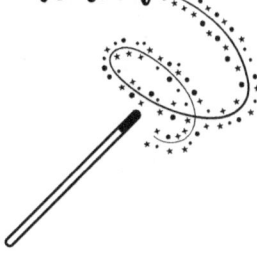

CAPRICORN
potion bag

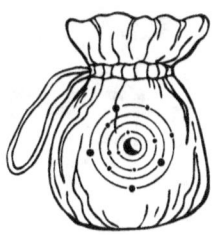

PISCES
athame

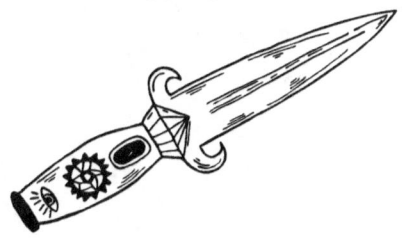

YOUR SIGN AS
nature

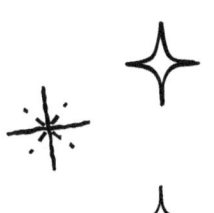
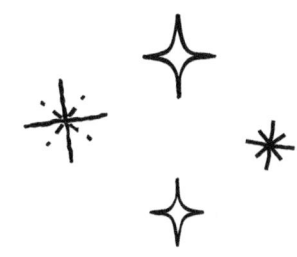

ARIES
volcano

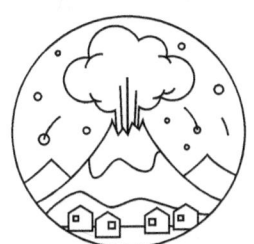

TAURUS
mountains

SAGITTARIUS
fjords

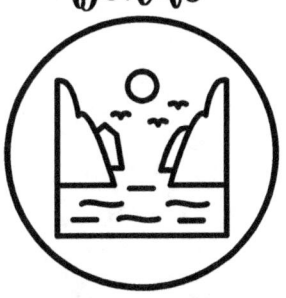

LEO
sunsets

CANCER
wildflowers

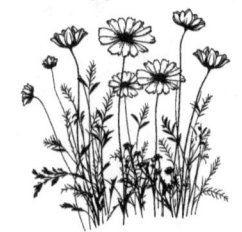

GEMINI
iceberg

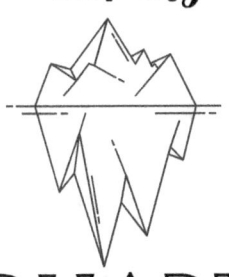

LIBRA
clouds

SCORPIO
coral reefs

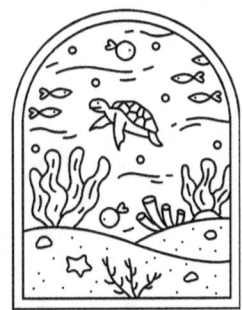

AQUARIUS
waterfalls

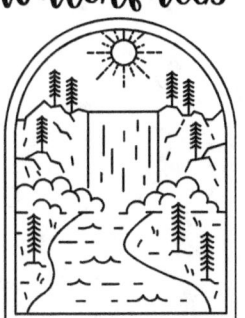

VIRGO
forests

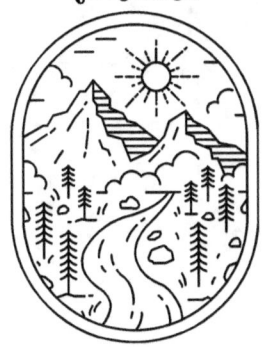

CAPRICORN
lightning

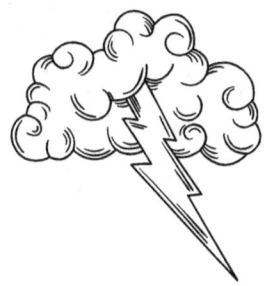

PISCES
beaches

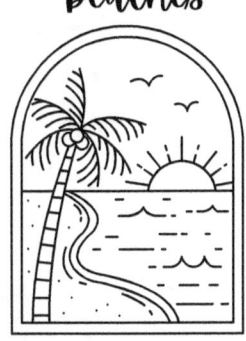

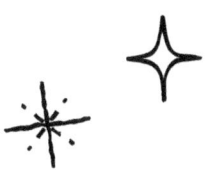

YOUR SIGN AS A
vacation spot

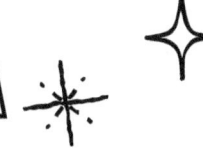
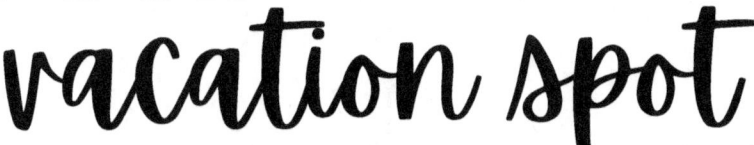
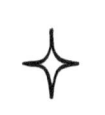

ARIES
Kauai

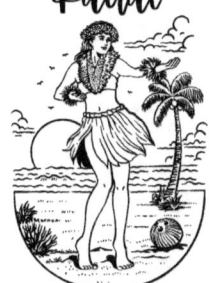

TAURUS
Paris

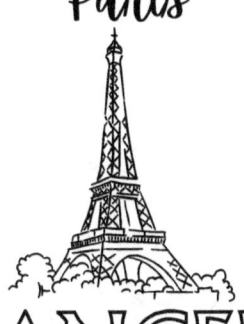

SAGITTARIUS
Mexico

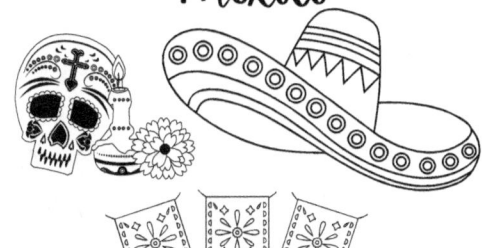

LEO
Maldives

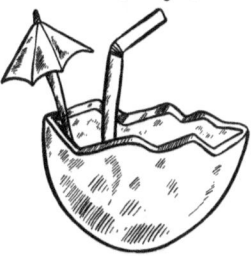

CANCER
Santorini

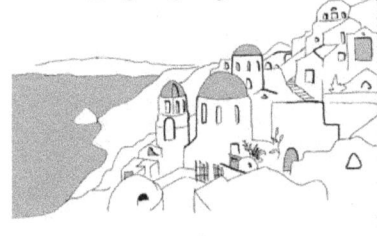

GEMINI
Galapagos Islands

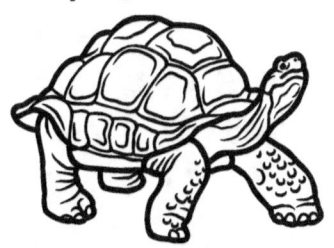

LIBRA
Venice

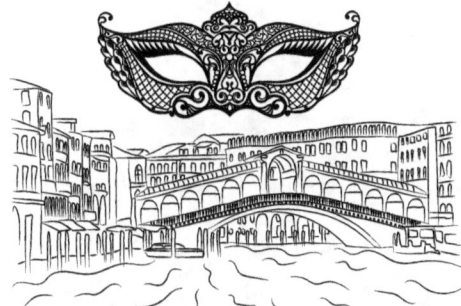

SCORPIO
Thailand

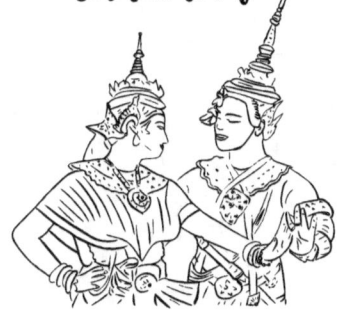

AQUARIUS
Japan

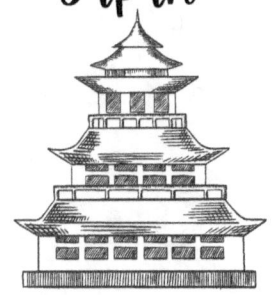

VIRGO
Tuscany

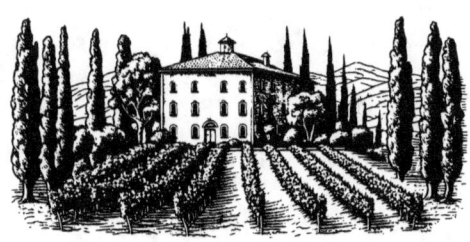

CAPRICORN
Shanghai

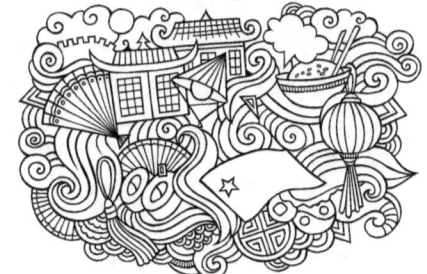

PISCES
Bahamas

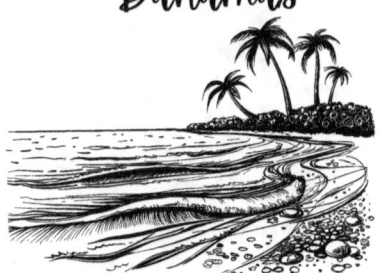

YOUR SIGN AS A
stress reducer

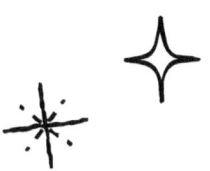
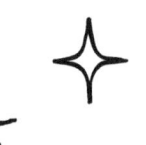

ARIES
going for a run

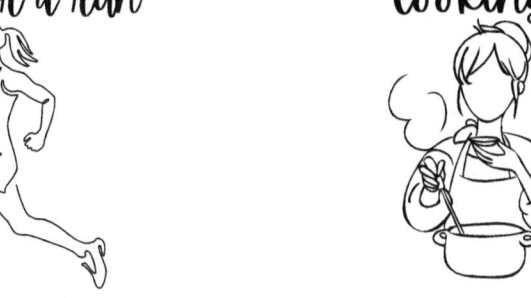

TAURUS
cooking

SAGITTARIUS
meditation

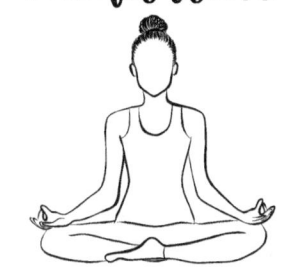

LEO
creating

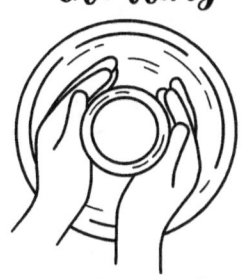

CANCER
baths

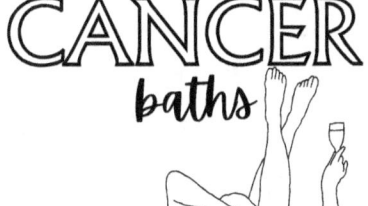
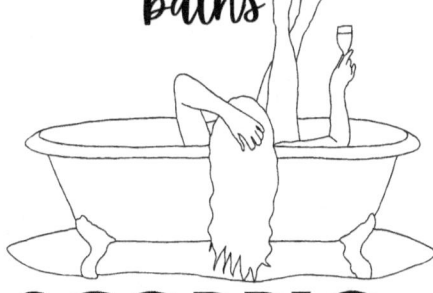

GEMINI
games

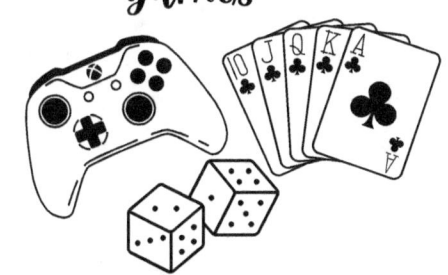

LIBRA
yoga

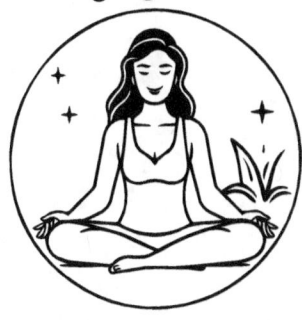

SCORPIO
music

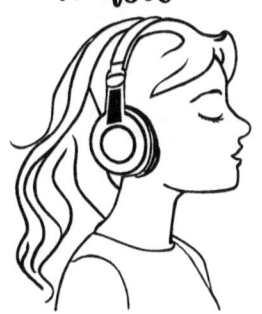

AQUARIUS
movie night

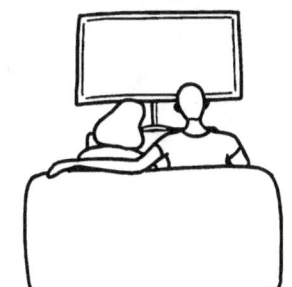

VIRGO
reading

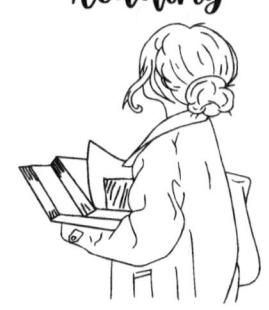

CAPRICORN
get outside

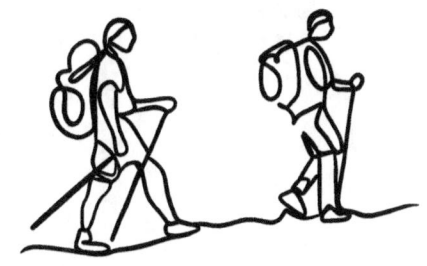

PISCES
aromatherapy

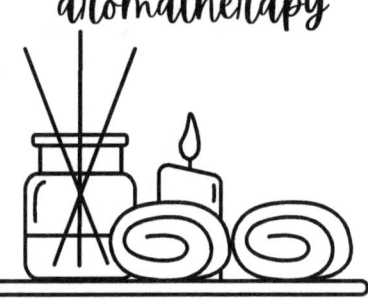

YOUR SIGN AS A
house

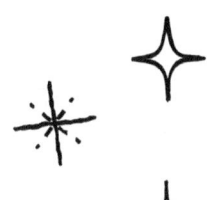

ARIES
apartment building

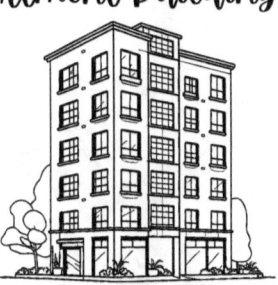

TAURUS
classic bungalow

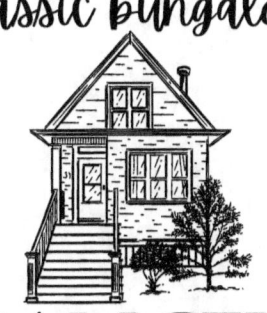

SAGITTARIUS
triple decker

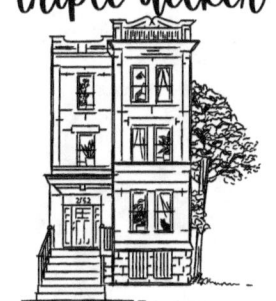

LEO
Victorian

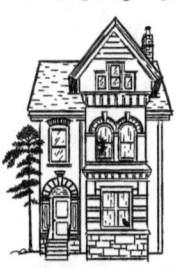

CANCER
cozy cottage

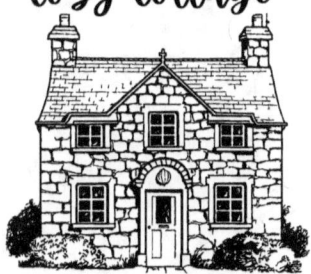

GEMINI
craftsman

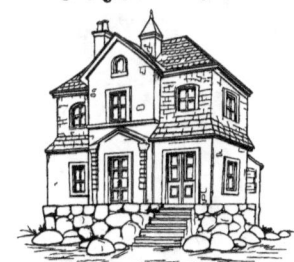

LIBRA
brick house

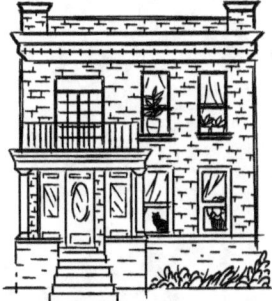

SCORPIO
secluded beach house

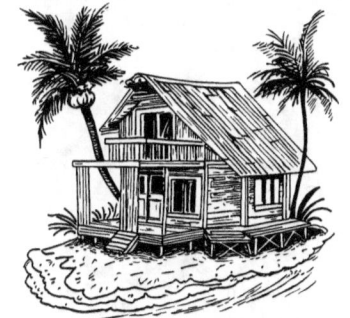

AQUARIUS
farmhouse

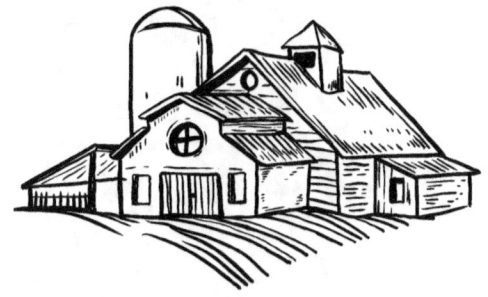

VIRGO
mid century modern

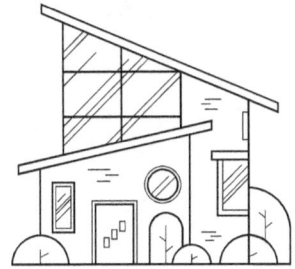

CAPRICORN
log cabin

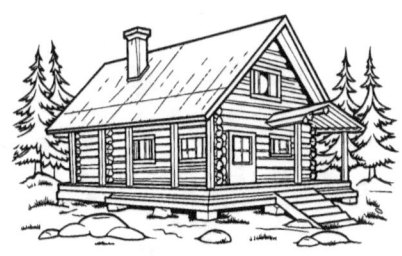

PISCES
haunted house

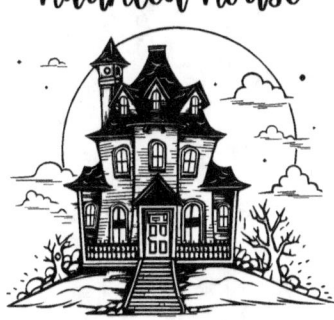

YOUR SIGN AS A
hobby

ARIES
calligraphy

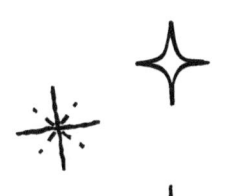

TAURUS
candlemaking

SAGITTARIUS
cake decorating

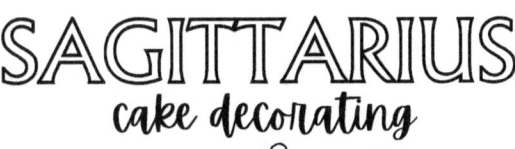

LEO
tie-dying

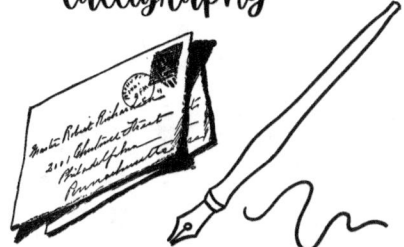

CANCER
scrapbooking

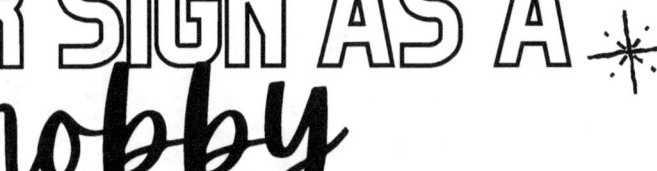

GEMINI
gardening

LIBRA
knitting

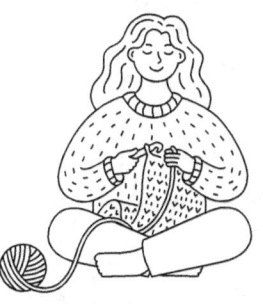

SCORPIO
jewelry making

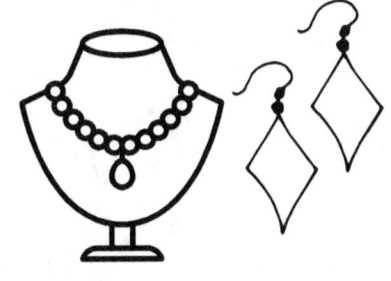

AQUARIUS
baking

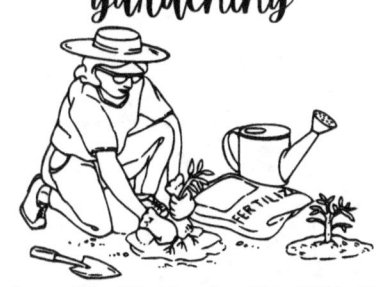

VIRGO
quilting

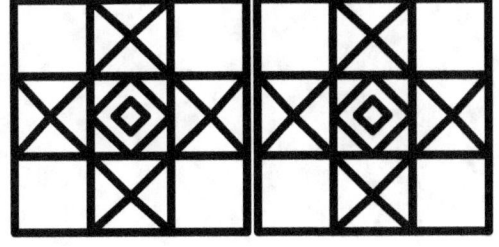

CAPRICORN
at home manicures

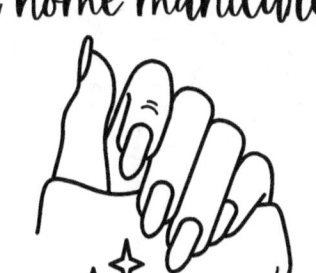

PISCES
pottery

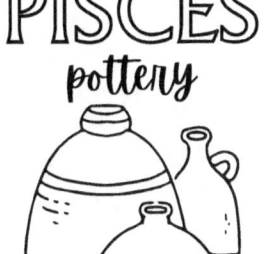

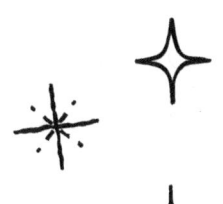 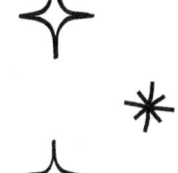

YOUR SIGN AS A
breakfast

ARIES
hash browns

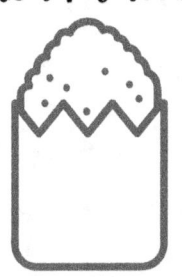

TAURUS
pancakes

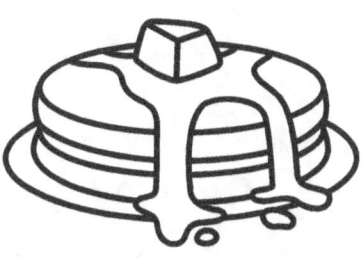

SAGITTARIUS
breakfast burrito

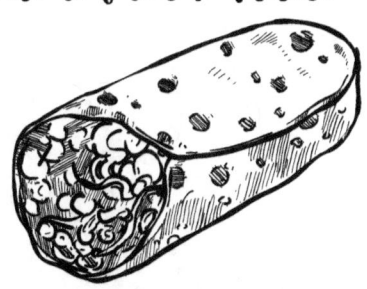

LEO
avocado toast

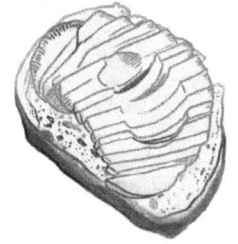

CANCER
yogurt parfait

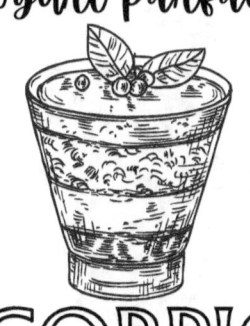

GEMINI
cereal

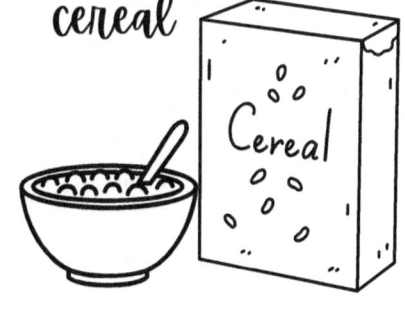

LIBRA
waffles

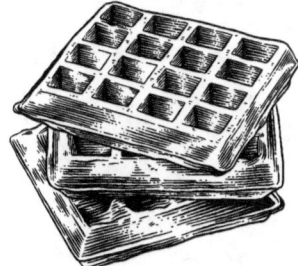

SCORPIO
french toast

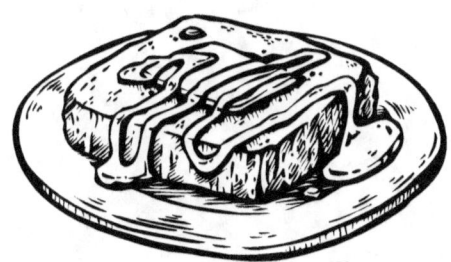

AQUARIUS
veggie omlet

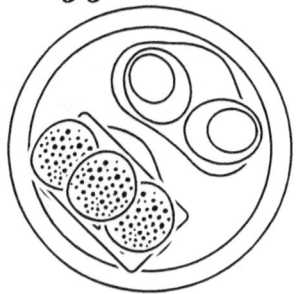

VIRGO
just coffee

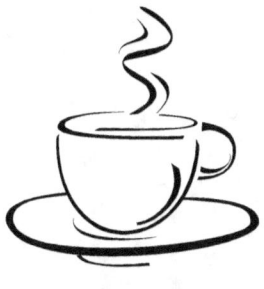

CAPRICORN
fancy oatmeal

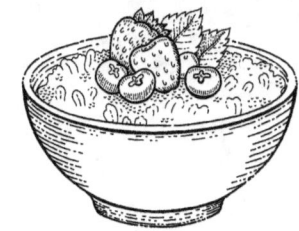

PISCES
cinnamon rolls

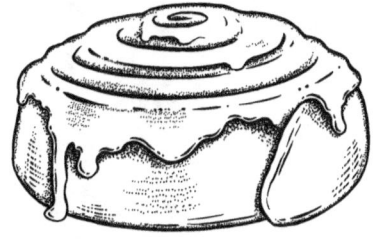

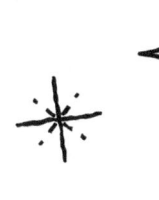 # YOUR SIGN AS AN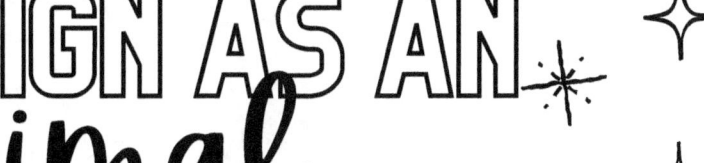
animal

ARIES
fox

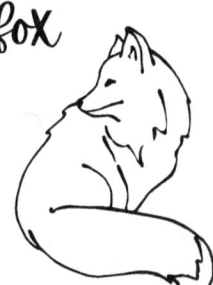

TAURUS
swan
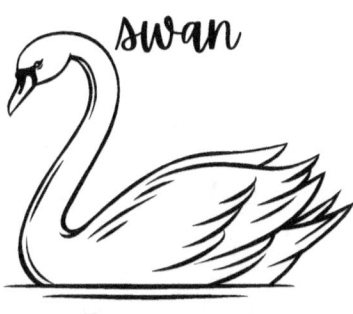

SAGITTARIUS
owl
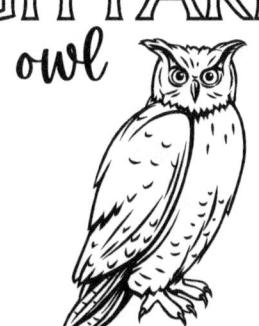

LEO
leopard
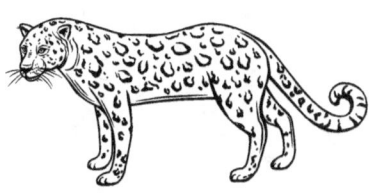

CANCER
rabbit
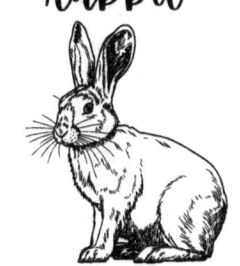

GEMINI
deer
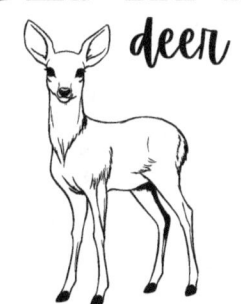

LIBRA
dolphin
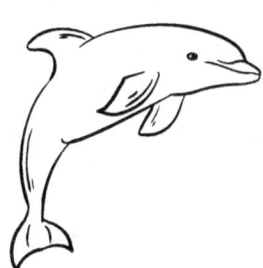

SCORPIO
snake
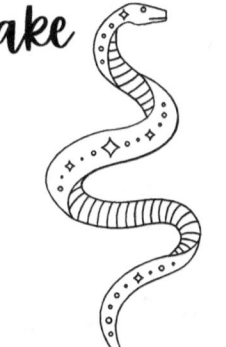

AQUARIUS
wolf
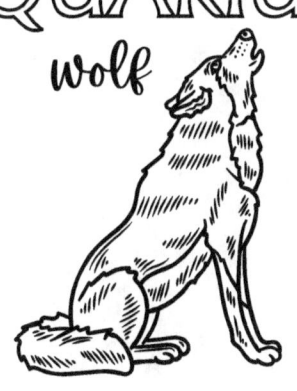

VIRGO
otter
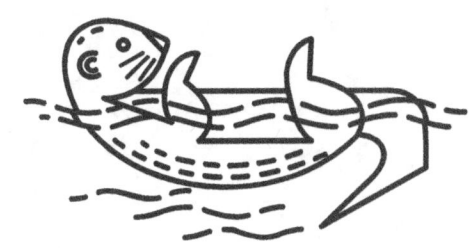

CAPRICORN
eagle
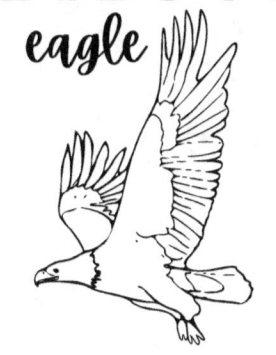

PISCES
unicorn
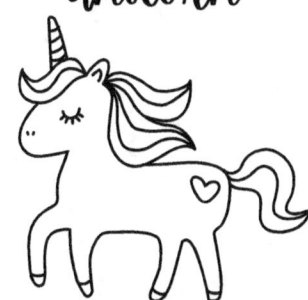

YOUR SIGN AS A
color

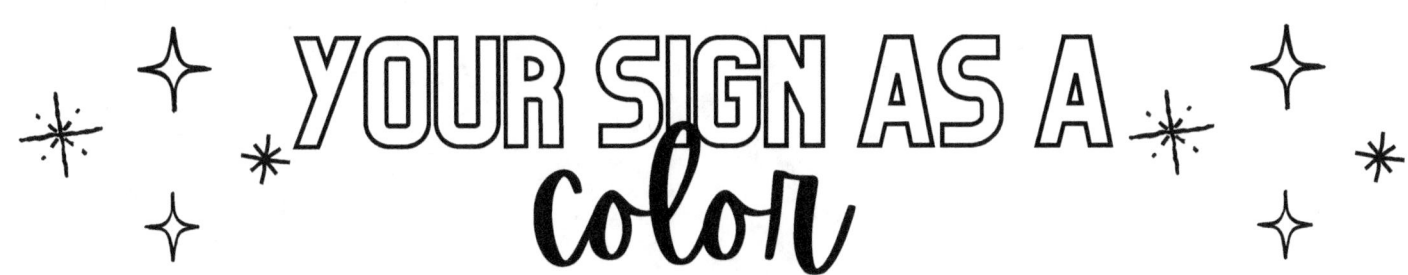

ARIES
shades of red

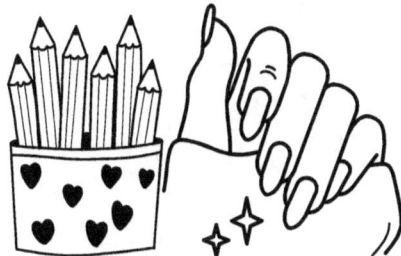

TAURUS
shades of pink

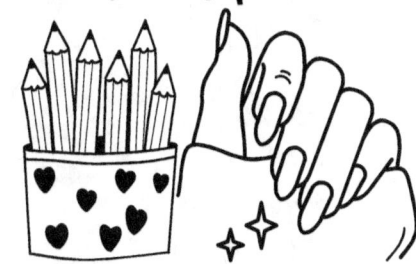

SAGITTARIUS
shades of purple

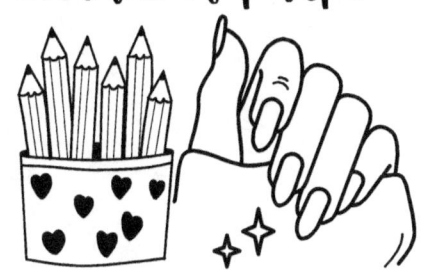

LEO
shades of orange & gold

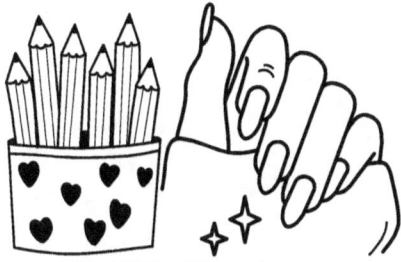

CANCER
shades of white & silver

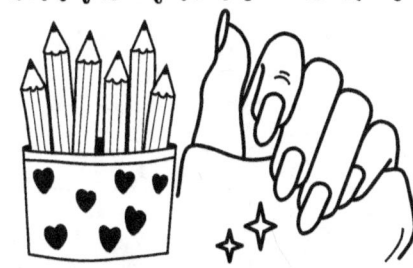

GEMINI
shades of yellow

LIBRA
pastels

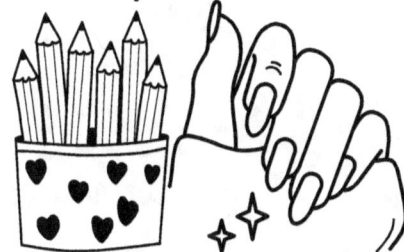

SCORPIO
shades of green

AQUARIUS
shades of blue

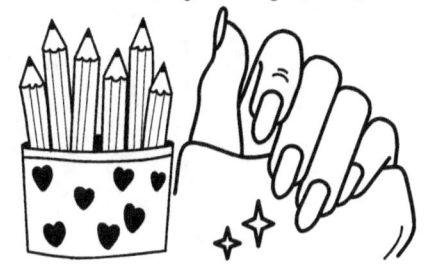

VIRGO
earth tones

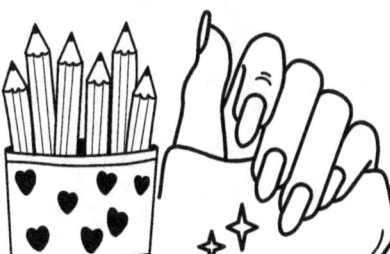

CAPRICORN
jewel tones

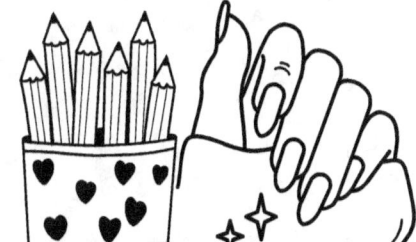

PISCES
cool tones

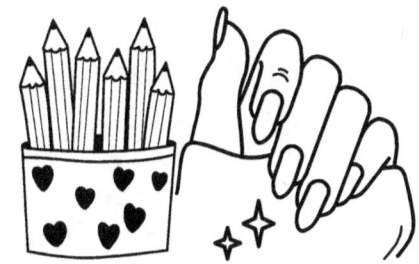

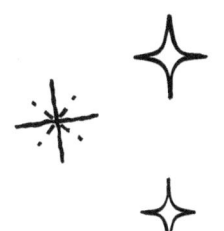 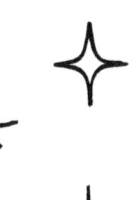 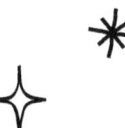

YOUR SIGN AS A
book genre

ARIES
romcom

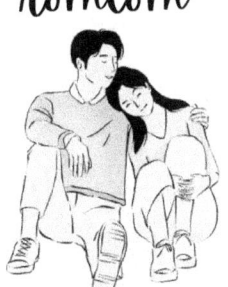

TAURUS
paranormal

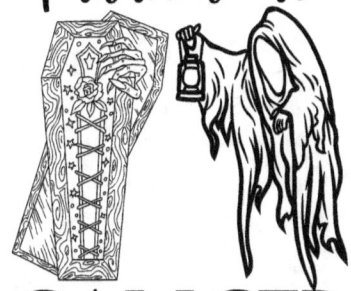

SAGITTARIUS
dystopian

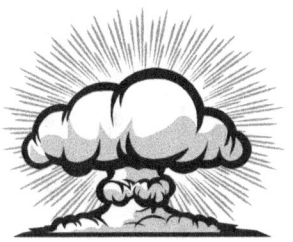

LEO
fantasy

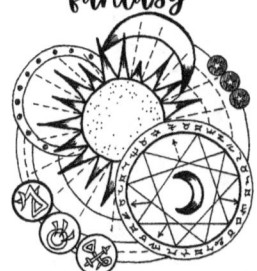

CANCER
historical

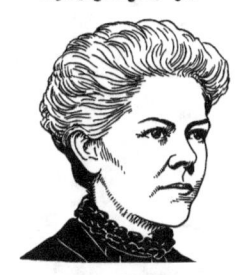

GEMINI
thriller

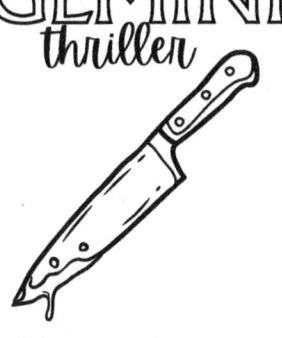

LIBRA
retelling

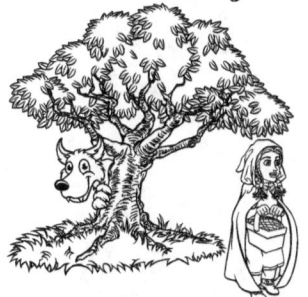

SCORPIO
horror

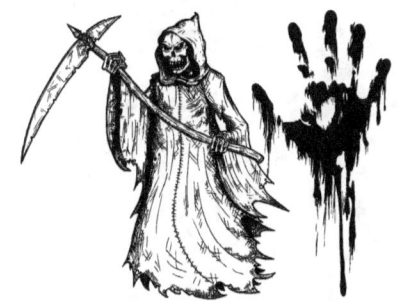

AQUARIUS
steampunk

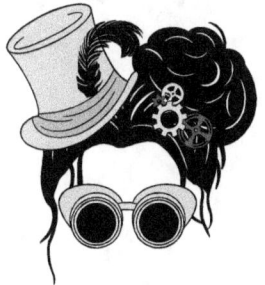

VIRGO
contemporary

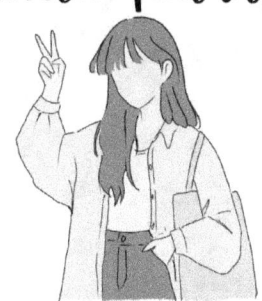

CAPRICORN
sci-fi

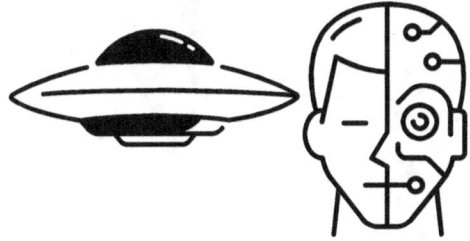

PISCES
tragedy

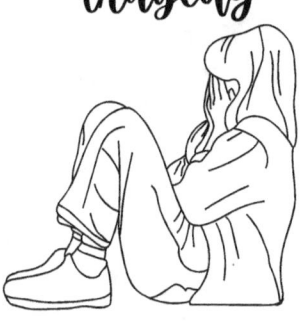

YOUR SIGN AS A
bird

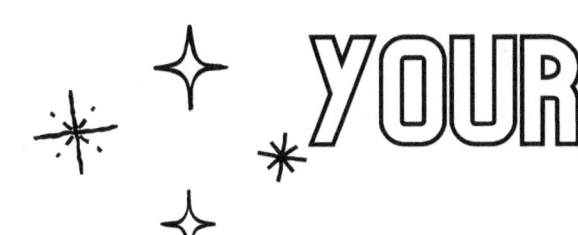

ARIES
hummingbird

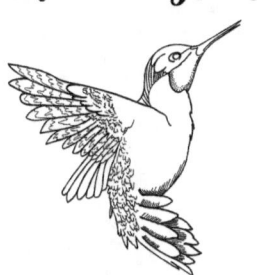

TAURUS
penguin

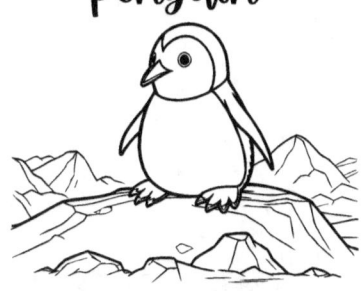

SAGITTARIUS
parrot

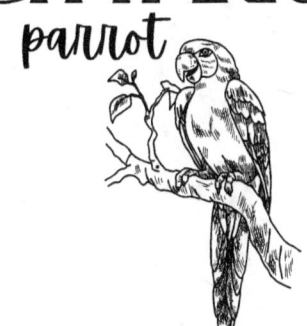

LEO
peacock

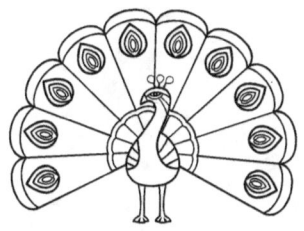

CANCER
dove

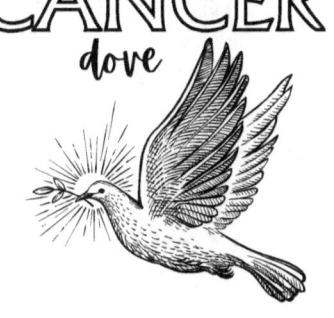

GEMINI
toucan

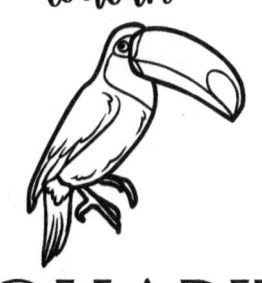

LIBRA
flamingo

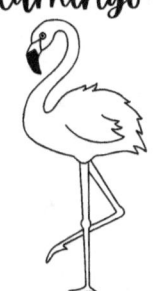

SCORPIO
swan

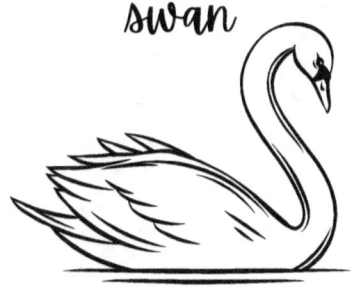

AQUARIUS
blue footed booby

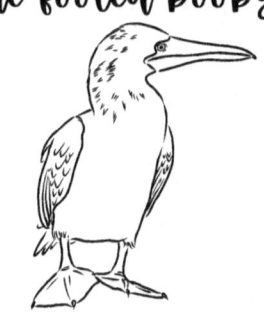

VIRGO
mandarin duck

CAPRICORN
woodpecker

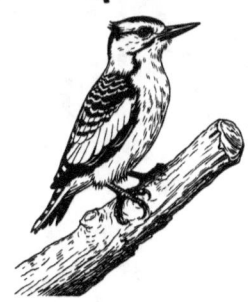

PISCES
owl

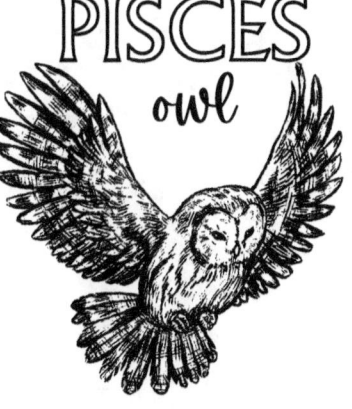

YOUR SIGN AS AN
aesthetic sticker

ARIES
just peachy

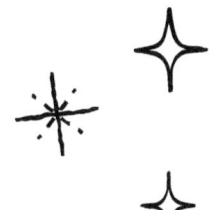

TAURUS
smores

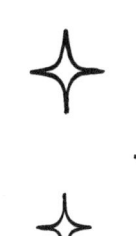

SAGITTARIUS
80's retro

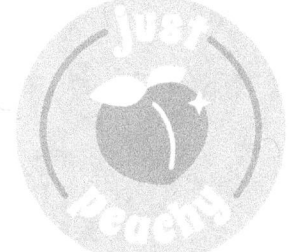

LEO
bubble gum

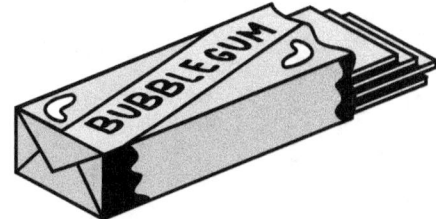

CANCER
balloon animal

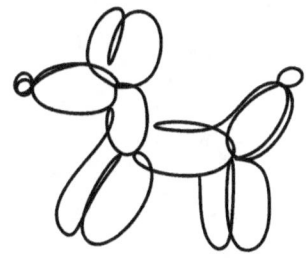

GEMINI
toaster

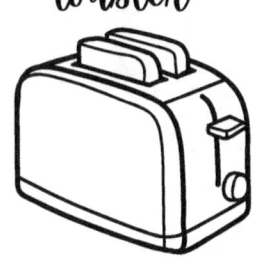

LIBRA
pretzel

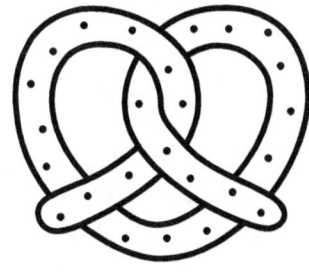

SCORPIO
sushi

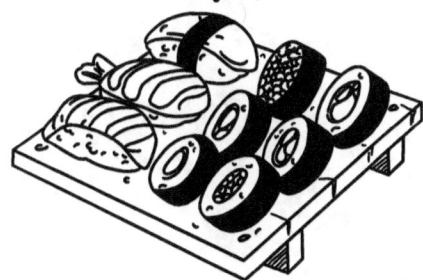

AQUARIUS
cowgirl hat

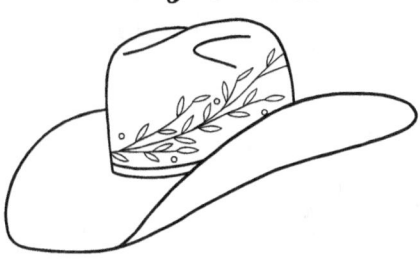

VIRGO
crocs

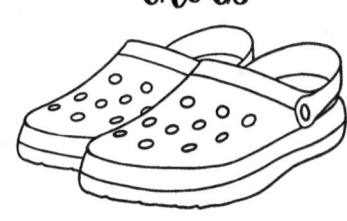

CAPRICORN
camera

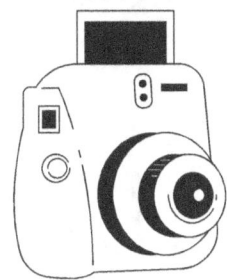

PISCES
tumbler

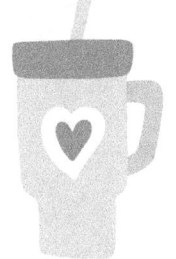

YOUR SIGN AS A
neon light

ARIES
lightning

TAURUS
hand love sign

SAGITTARIUS
flamingo

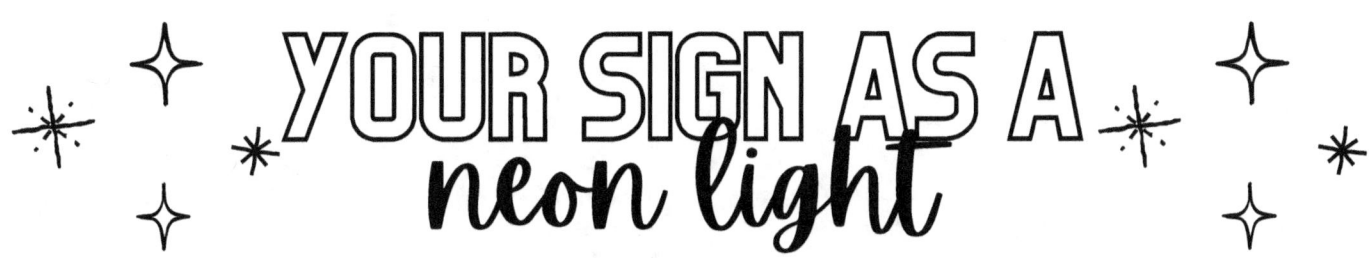

LEO
outer space

CANCER
Love

GEMINI
microphone

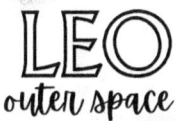

LIBRA
rose

SCORPIO
cactus

AQUARIUS
rocket

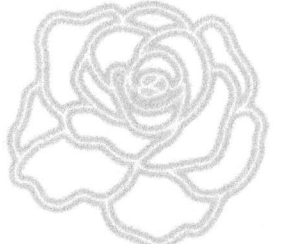

VIRGO
game on

CAPRICORN
cheers

PISCES
peace

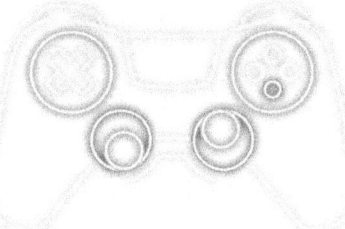

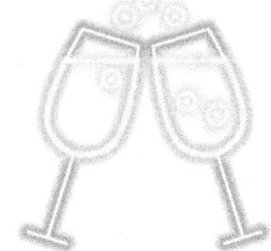

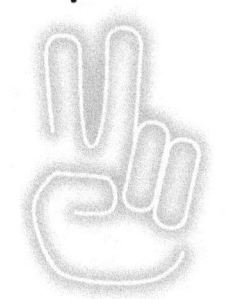

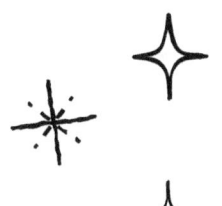 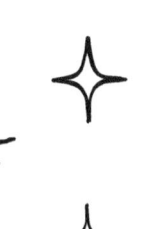 

YOUR SIGN AS A
Halloween costume

ARIES
devil

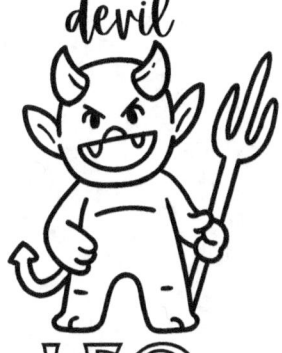

TAURUS
black cat

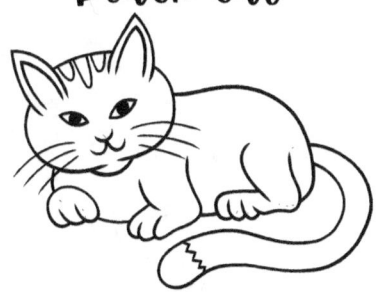

SAGITTARIUS
pirate

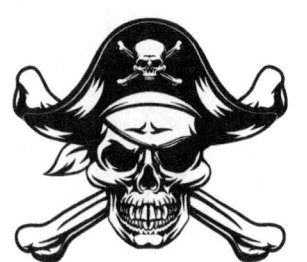

LEO
superhero

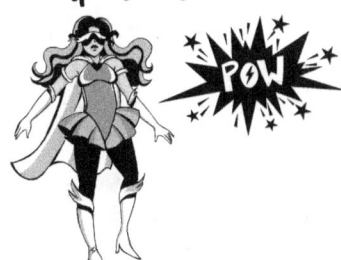

CANCER
ghost

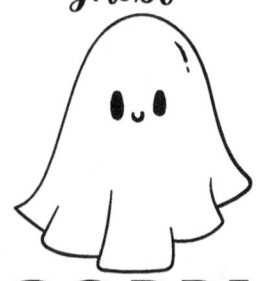

GEMINI
warewolf

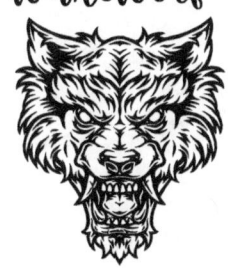

LIBRA
angel

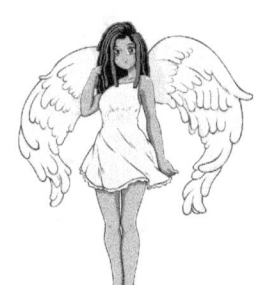

SCORPIO
vampire

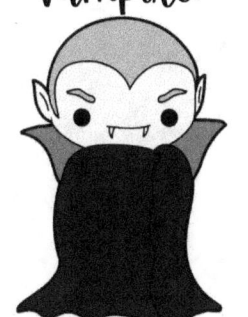

AQUARIUS
alien

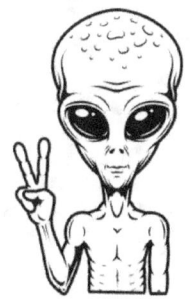

VIRGO
nurse

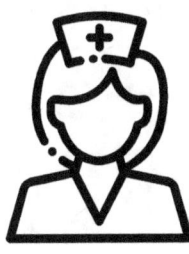

CAPRICORN
mummy

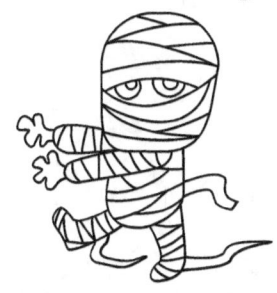

PISCES
witch

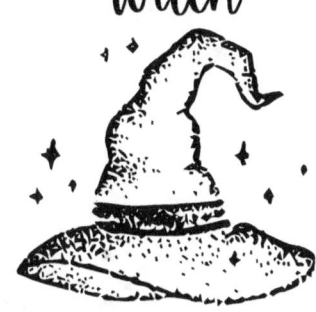

YOUR SIGN AS
autumn time

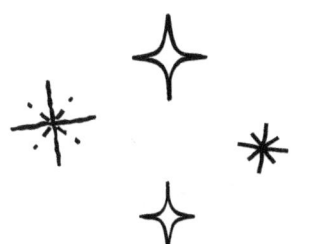 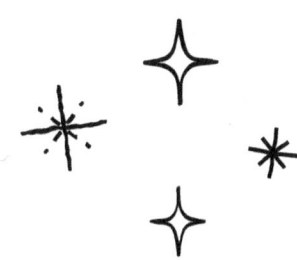

ARIES
apple picking

TAURUS
baking pies
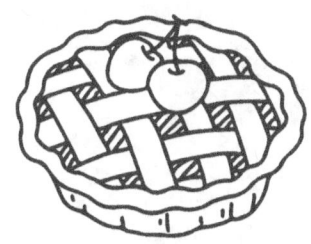

SAGITTARIUS
corn maze
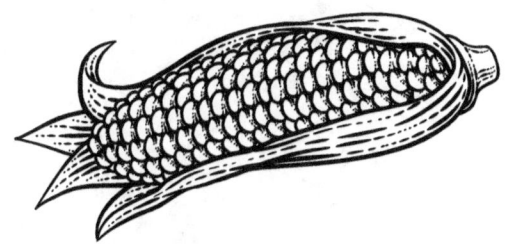

LEO
pumpkin spice latte

CANCER
cozy sweater
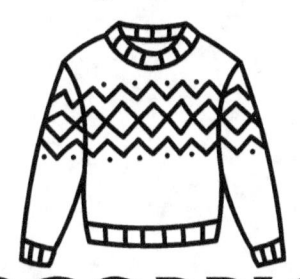

GEMINI
fireside reading
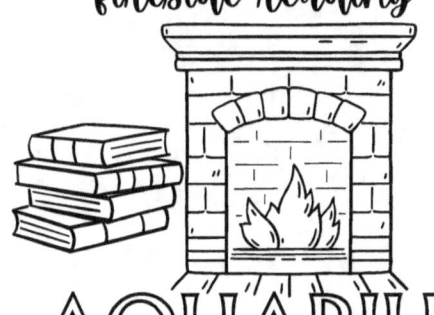

LIBRA
autumn decor

SCORPIO
Halloween everything
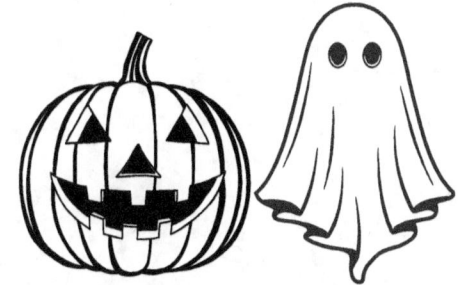

AQUARIUS
candy corn
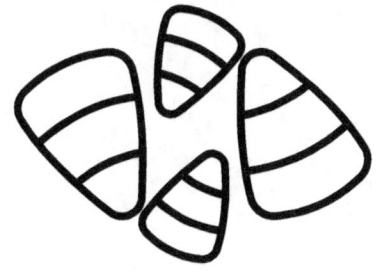

VIRGO
pumpkin patch

CAPRICORN
homemade soup
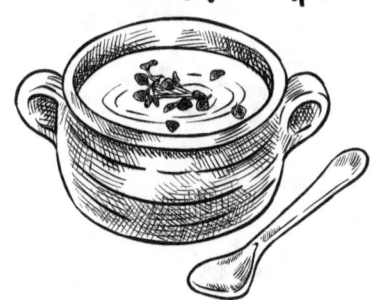

PISCES
caramel apples
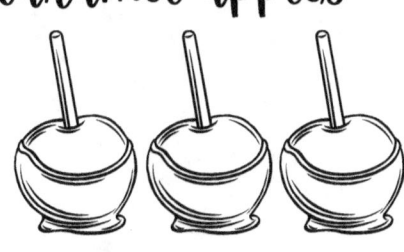

YOUR SIGN AS
winter time

ARIES
mittens and hats

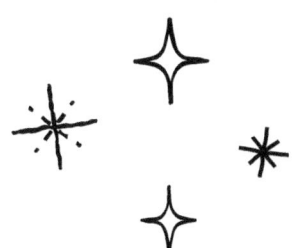

TAURUS
building a snowman

SAGITTARIUS
snow angels

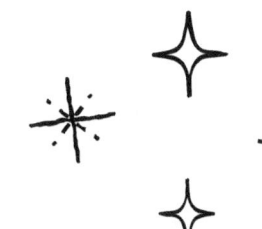

LEO
putting up Christmas lights

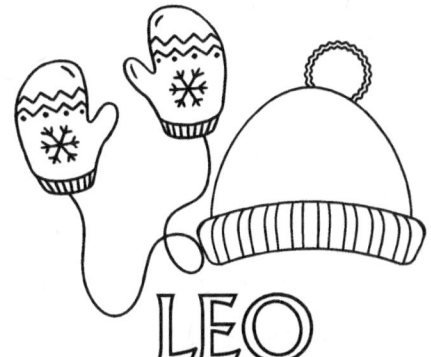

CANCER
writing Christmas cards

GEMINI
snowball fights

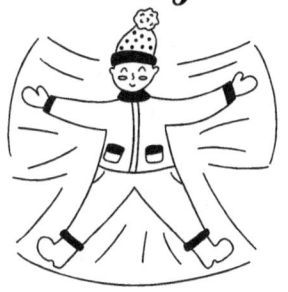

LIBRA
reading books by the fire

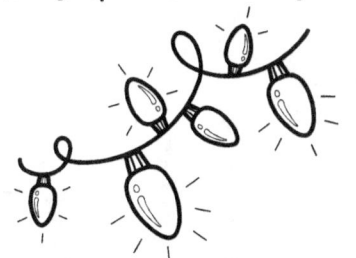

SCORPIO
wintry hike

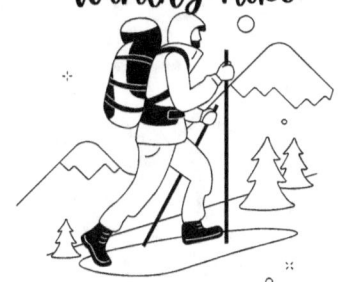

AQUARIUS
jigsaw puzzles

VIRGO
ice skating

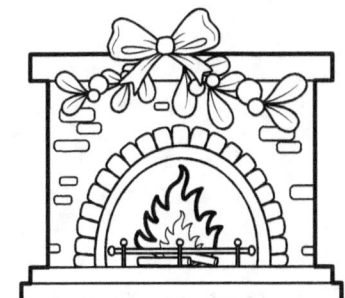

CAPRICORN
New Years Eve Bash

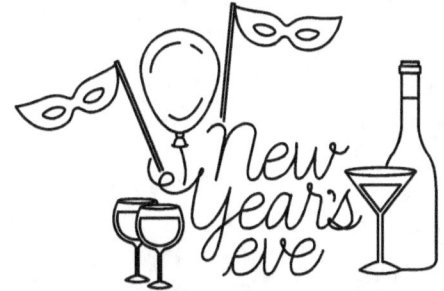

PISCES
making a gingerbread house

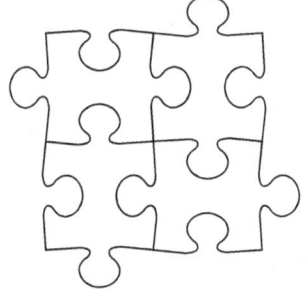

YOUR SIGN AS
spring time

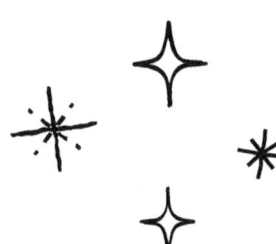
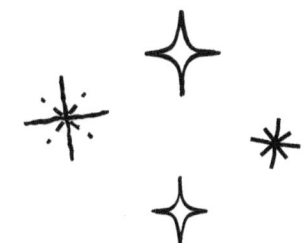

ARIES
bird watching

TAURUS
bike rides

SAGITTARIUS
hiking

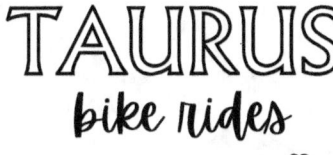
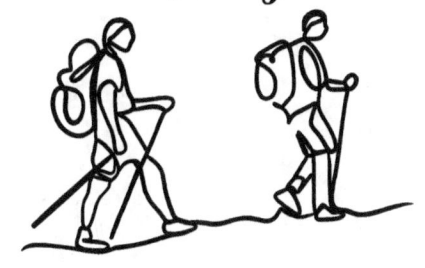

LEO
outdoor yoga

CANCER
planting a garden

GEMINI
spring festival

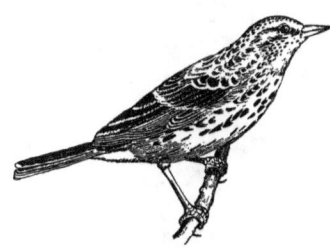
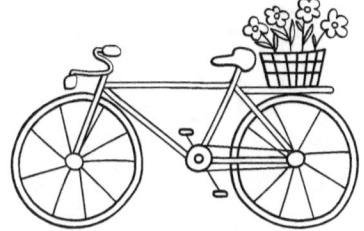

LIBRA
deep spring clean

SCORPIO
picnic in the park

AQUARIUS
farmers markets

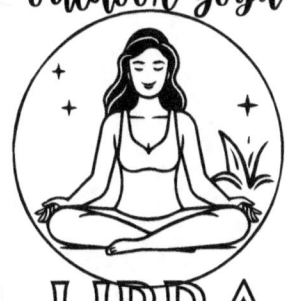
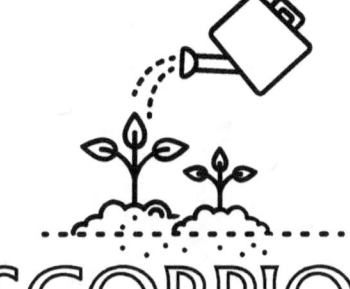
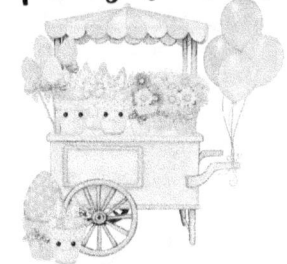

VIRGO
zoo visit

CAPRICORN
easter egg hunt

PISCES
volunteering

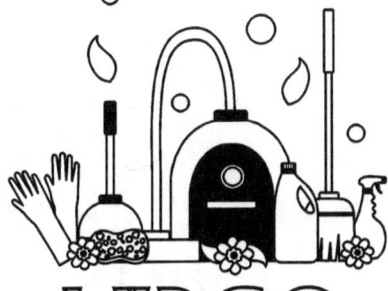
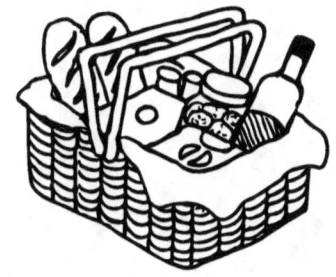
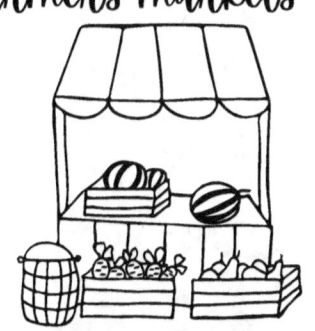
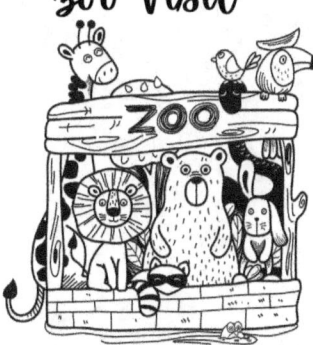
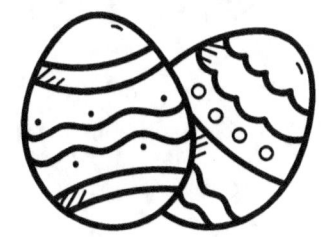

YOUR SIGN AS
summertime

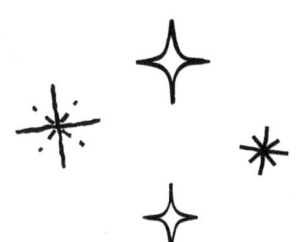
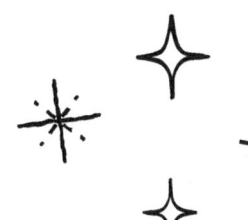

ARIES
amusement park ride

TAURUS
tanning

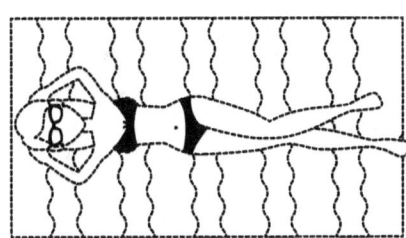

SAGITTARIUS
camping

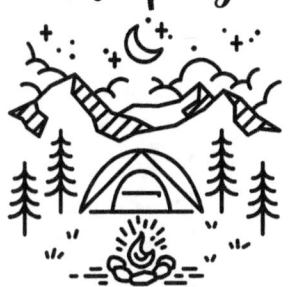

LEO
berry picking

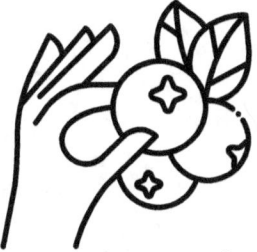

CANCER
hitting the garage sales

GEMINI
roadtrips

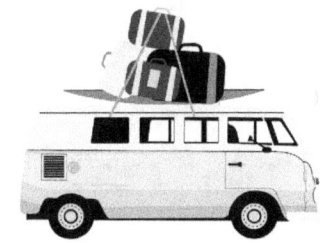

LIBRA
4th of july fireworks

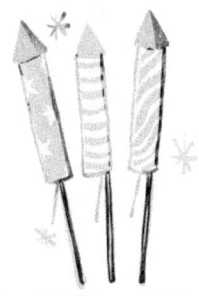

SCORPIO
movies in the park

AQUARIUS
outdoor concert

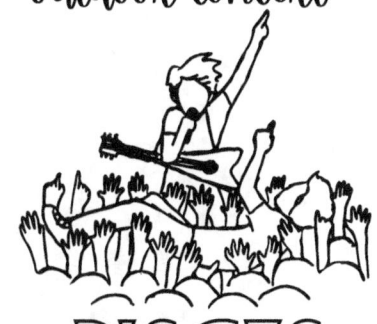

VIRGO
beach day

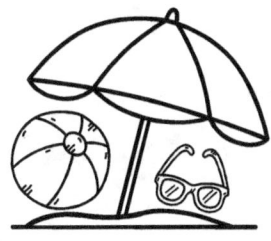

CAPRICORN
neighborhood barbeque

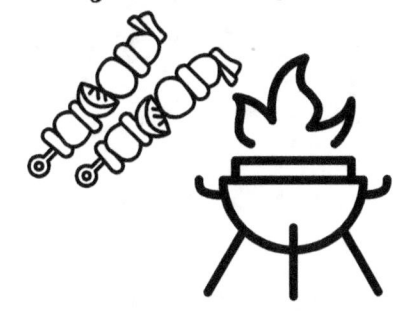

PISCES
ice cream truck

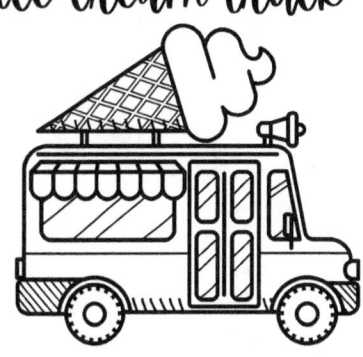

YOUR SIGN AS
self care

ARIES
sweat it out

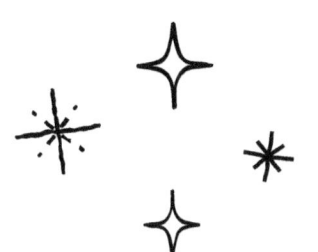

TAURUS
cooking | baking

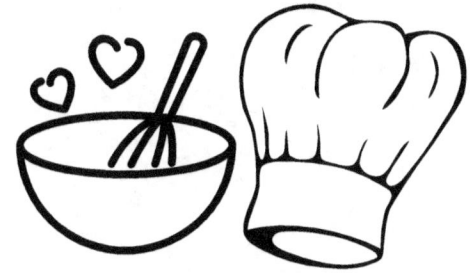

SAGITTARIUS
plan a trip

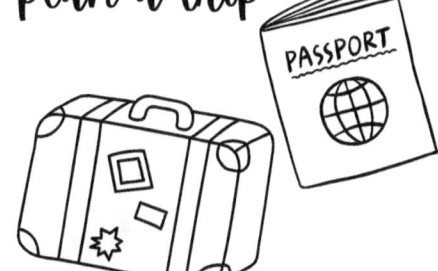

LEO
have fun

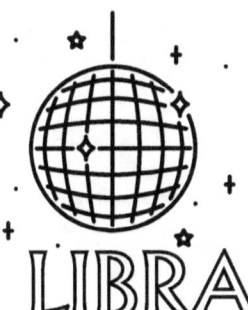

CANCER
take a bath

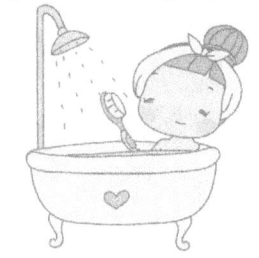

GEMINI
journal

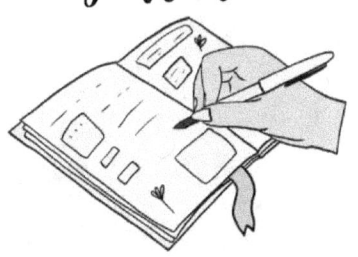

LIBRA
feng shui your space

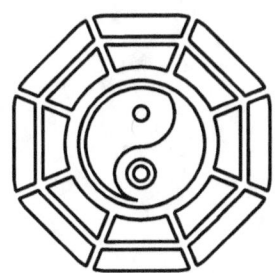

SCORPIO
create art

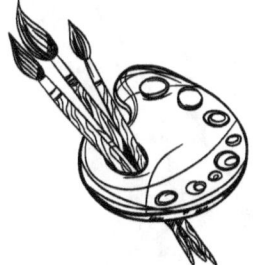

AQUARIUS
crystal therapy

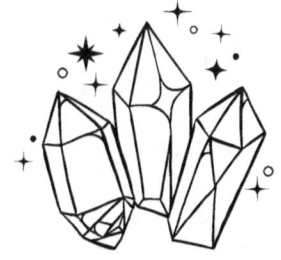

VIRGO
organize

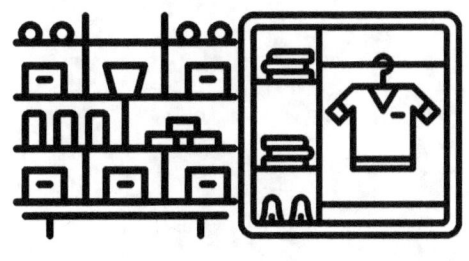

CAPRICORN
meditate

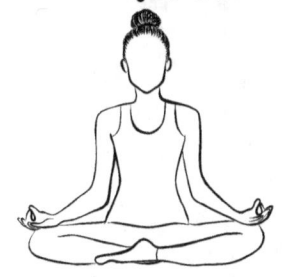

PISCES
write poetry

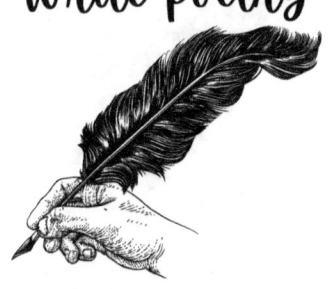

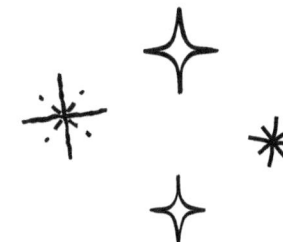
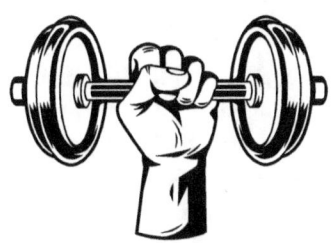